——— THE ———
Afterlife

THE
Afterlife

What *Really* Happens in the Hereafter

Elizabeth Clare Prophet

SUMMIT UNIVERSITY PRESS®

Gardiner, Montana

THE AFTERLIFE: What *Really* Happens in the Hereafter
by Elizabeth Clare Prophet
Copyright © 2020 The Summit Lighthouse, Inc.
All rights reserved

For information:
Summit University Press
63 Summit Way, Gardiner, MT 59030 USA
1-800-245-5445 / 406-848-9500
SummitUniversityPress.com

Library of Congress Control Number: 2019944000
ISBN: 978-1-60988-316-4 (softbound)
ISBN: 978-1-60988-317-1 (eBook)

SUMMIT UNIVERSITY ☙ PRESS®

Disclaimer and Notes: (1) No guarantee whatsoever is made to anyone by Summit University Press that the spiritual practice of the science of the spoken Word, including meditation, visualization, dynamic decrees and spiritual healing discussed in this book will yield successful results for anyone at any time. The spiritual practices described in this book do not replace medical treatment or diagnosis. The practice and proof of the science of being rests with the individual. (2) Because gender-neutral language can be cumbersome and at times confusing, we have often used *he* and *him* to refer to God or to the individual. These terms are for readability only and are not intended to exclude women or the feminine aspect of the Divine. (3) The soul of man and woman is feminine in relation to the masculine, or spirit, portion of being. The soul is therefore sometimes referred to as *she.* (4) Some details of the true stories in this book have been omitted or changed to protect the privacy of the individuals. The story "A Classic Love Triangle through the Centuries" is fictional, written to illustrate karma and reincarnation.

23 22 21 20   1 2 3 4

Contents

Chapter 3

Chapter 4

Chapter 5
TAKING HEAVEN BY FORCE 97

Chapter 6
COMMANDING THE LIGHT 121

A Handbook for Understanding and Preparing for the Afterlife

You may have picked up this book because you've just lost someone close to you or you know someone who is terminally ill and you're looking for answers, comfort, and reassurance. Perhaps you've read a book on near-death experiences and still have questions. What *really* happens when we die and who will we see on the other side? Is it as simple as a one-way trip to heaven or hell? What comes next—and why?

There is a large and varied field of literature on the subject of the afterlife. Many, if not most, of these books are an exploration of the world beyond gleaned from the captivating stories of near-death experiences, or NDEs, told by those who have experienced a taste of the afterlife and have come back to tell us about their voyages of discovery.

This diverse group includes a marine sniper (Dannion Brinkley, *Saved by the Light*), a Christian (Betty J. Eadie, *Embraced by the Light*), a neurosurgeon (Eben Alexander, *Proof of Heaven*), and the survivor of an attempted suicide (Angie Fenimore, *Beyond the Darkness*), among many others. Some researchers have catalogued the NDEs of children. Others have compiled near-encyclopedic accounts of people of all ages, gender, cultures, and religions who have had strikingly similar NDEs.

Taken as a whole, books on near-death experiences have documented the ongoing nature of the soul and provided glimpses into the afterlife—the key word being *glimpses.* Which brings us to the purpose of this volume.

This book picks up where others leave off. Going well beyond the unplanned, minutes-long visits to spiritual dimensions by "accidental tourists" who have had NDEs, it provides expert information about the afterlife. Simply stated, *The Afterlife: What* Really *Happens in the Hereafter* is a handbook that will help you prepare for the most important journey you will ever take: your journey to the afterlife. It gives essential insights into what happens at the end of life and why. It then goes on to offer tools and techniques you can use to arrive at the best destination for you.

Who could write such a book? Elizabeth Clare Prophet is one of the few who has the inner sight and depth of spiritual understanding to explain these "mysteries," and she does so in a way that is so accessible and down-to-earth that anyone can understand them. Drawn from several lectures she gave on the afterlife, this illuminating work provides a unique tool kit and the spiritual know-how to help everyone find their way into the light.

Prophet was at the forefront of the body-mind-spirit movement as a teacher, author, and visionary. She devoted her life to helping people understand the inner realities of the world we live in and the world beyond, showing them how to embrace life's opportunities and deal with its obstacles in a way that is both liberating and comforting.

All writers have a philosophy that guides their views. Prophet's philosophy is eclectic, drawing on truth from wherever she finds it in the world's spiritual traditions as well as from her own perceptive understanding of life. She conveys that wisdom with a compassion and practicality that allows readers of any faith or tradition, or none at all, to apply it to their own chosen path. In this book she builds on the understanding of those who have gone before her and explains the spiritual realms from the point of view of those who have "permanent residency" —those enlightened beings who have graduated from earth's schoolroom and with whom she has a deep spiritual connection.

In these pages, you'll find rare insights into the architecture of the many dimensions of the afterlife—from the higher, "etheric," levels of consciousness (what is commonly called heaven) to the lower levels of illusion and darkness. You'll read her astute commentary on NDEs as introduced in the works of Dr. Raymond Moody, who coined the term NDE, and others. And you'll gain a deeper knowledge of the laws of life from her analysis of popular movies that deal with the afterlife.

But that's just a start. You'll also learn about the real purpose of the "life review" (and "pre-life review"), the factors of karma and reincarnation, the special "spiritual retreats" in the heaven world where souls may be escorted after death to heal from traumatic events, and how we can assist those who are having a hard time moving on. You'll learn about "discarnates" (or "bewildered spirits," as Dr. Moody calls them), which Prophet says are realistically portrayed in the movie *Ghost,* and you'll discover ways to protect yourself and others from their negative influence.

Elizabeth Clare Prophet also tackles key misconceptions about the afterlife, compassionately dispelling the simplistic notions of heaven and hell that too often cause us to live in fear instead of peace. Importantly, she reveals that we are in charge of shaping our future by the choices we make today. How we live and what we do now sets the course for our journey in the afterlife. When all is said and done, this essential guide to the afterlife will give you the understanding, support, and spiritual tools to prepare for your own ultimate journey—and to navigate the path ahead with confidence.

Summit University Press

CHAPTER 1

Understanding the Continuity of Life

The unconscious psyche believes in life after death.

CARL G. JUNG, SWISS PSYCHOANALYST

You have lived in the infinite past. You will live in the infinite future. And therefore the cessation of life in the physical body need not be of concern to you. What is worthy of your greatest concern is that you will have accomplished everything you want to do—for God, for yourself, for your family, for your community, for your favorite causes for humanity—before that body runs out of steam and gives up the ghost, so to speak. Yet as we see in the news each day, one never knows when this life's opportunity may be cut short for ourselves or for our loved ones.

Preoccupation with death is the preoccupation with something that is not real. Death is not real. That is what near-death experiences, often called NDEs, tell us. *Death* is the name given to the process whereby the systems of the physical body shut down—the brain, the heart, and the rest following. But it's not a cessation of life or consciousness or the continuity of your soul.

It's not that you cease to exist. It's not that you're going to heaven or you're going to hell. *It's that you no longer have a physical body.* That is the major adjustment.

At this point of shedding the physical body, we have already set the stage for what happens next. Throughout our lives, every thought we think, every emotion we feel, every action we take is done with God's energy. We perform our actions and deeds by the waterfall of light that comes from our Divine Source into our hearts. And when we receive this energy, it is a crystal clear stream of the water of Life.

We then qualify this stream either with purity or we qualify it with negatives such as envy, anger, fear, doubt, and depression. These discordant vibrations burden others. They also burden us and create an accumulation of negativity. And that negativity will sit there until we turn our hatreds into loves, our hardness of heart into mercy and forgiveness, our warlike energies into peace. Our qualification of God's energy is cumulative throughout our lifetimes and determines much of what happens to us between lives.

It's very important that we understand this process. There are many variables that determine what happens after you leave the body at the transition called death. I want to acquaint you with a number of possibilities—and potential pitfalls. I will also explain what you need to know to prepare for them. When you pass on, the vast majority of you will be entering an interim period where you are preparing once again to be on the scene in your next life. A small percentage of people will have fulfilled their reason for being on earth. They will not return but will move on in their spiritual evolution.

Your ultimate goal is to stop reincarnating by achieving union with your Higher Self and your God Presence. People who have had near-death experiences return with a sense of this divine union. They long to keep the bliss that they have experienced on the other side, even while they live out the rest of their renewed opportunity.

Where Do We Go and Why?

I have prayed for many souls after they have passed on, and I am often allowed to see what happens to them. At the conclusion of the Gulf War in the Middle East, I was praying for those who had passed on, not only Americans and our allied troops but those from every side—the Iraqis, everyone who had participated, and all those innocent civilians whose lives had been taken.

What I found was very interesting. The devout people, men and women in the armed forces, those of every nation who were truly spiritual and had led prayerful lives and devoted lives and had pure hearts, had already been taken by angels to spiritual retreats in the heaven-world. Some of them had such a momentum of light that they were already there. Others were of the light but were not able to get there, so I called to the angels to take these souls, who welcomed the angels and went with them. Some of the very devout Muslims, who were praying next to their bodies, couldn't get anywhere past their bodies. Where their dead bodies lay, there they were on their knees in prayer. They were in perpetual prayer and had been from the moment that they had been killed.

But then I saw a most interesting thing. I saw some soldiers (and they were from every nation, including our own) who had no desire to go into the realms of light. They were very angry that they had been killed, and they were expressing this anger in rage or in cursing or in foul words. They were putting out a tremendous amount of anger, and therefore they were not taken to a place of harmony or rest or learning. This was not only because they weren't fit to go there but because they actually denied the angels who came for them. These soldiers said that they did not want to go to a retreat of light where they could learn. This is a great pity because angels are surely our best friends.

So you can see that being involved in a war on either side did not determine where these souls found themselves after passing. Their state of consciousness did.

Your Afterlife Is Unique

I've observed all kinds of amazing conditions with individuals who have passed away. As I've said, some souls are taken directly to the heaven-world by angels right after they pass. They have such a momentum in their service and in their love of God that they have simply gravitated to the level that they are already native to.

Some souls go willingly with the angels when they arrive. They awaken, see the truth, and realize that they must go with the angels to higher realms, where they can do what they are supposed to be doing in the afterlife: preparing for rebirth.

But some people reject or ignore the angels because these individuals are much happier going on with whatever they are doing in the lower realms, levels of illusion that are not part of the heaven-world. Or they may be confused and think that they are still in a physical body because their surroundings may seem familiar. This can easily happen in the lower levels of the afterlife.

Some souls don't have enough spiritual attainment to make it to heavenly realms on their own. They must wait until someone on earth calls to the angels to go and rescue them.

I'd like to give you a few examples of people I have known and prayed for when they passed on from various causes in order to illustrate the great diversity of afterlife circumstances.

Trapped by Habit

A woman passed on at the age of sixty. She had had some dedication to the spiritual path for about four years. But when I made calls for her, I found her stuck in the lower realms of the afterlife. She was surrounded by sympathy and self-pity, and so she was tied to others there of the same vibration. She was sitting with a couple of gossiping ladies.

When I saw this, I projected my presence to her and said, "You must listen to me. You must go with the angels who have come to take you." She looked at me and at the angels and said, "Why are you here?" Then she remembered and said, "Oh, I know why you're here. I have to go with you." She turned to the other ladies and said, "I have to leave now. I'm going to a better place."

Now the other two ladies, who were there because of their own karma, said to her, "Uh huh. We'll see about that. You won't be happy there." They were trying to talk her out of going with the angels to the heaven-world! When people get stuck in the lower realms, there's a tremendous pull to keep them there.

Fortunately this woman chose to go with the angels. It gave her a good start for coming back in her next life and making progress on her spiritual path.

Terminal Cancer

There was a longtime member of my church who died of cancer at age sixty-five. She didn't have too much of a spiritual momentum in her fourteen years in our community. The last time I had seen her she looked well, but she told me at the time that she wasn't long for this world. She knew that she would reincarnate. When I prayed for her after she passed on, she was already in the heaven-world. She was attending classes there to prepare for her next life on earth.

Cocaine Overdose

I knew a young man who had come to the United States from South America. He had quit using marijuana and cocaine, but he later returned to South America and eventually passed on of a cocaine overdose. The overdose may have been an accident, or it may have been given to him by someone who intended to kill him. He was robbed after he died.

When I found out about his passing, I called to Archangel Michael and the blue-lightning angels to find him and to take him where he belonged. The lower levels where he was found, which are not part of the heaven-world, are what I define as the *astral plane*.* These lower levels have unfathomable depths of darkness, descending to levels that anyone would recognize as the traditional picture of hell. It is not easy to find people there.

I always ask the angels to take the person to the appropriate place of learning and preparation for their soul. Well, this young man was found sitting in a bar on the astral plane. He had been partying since he died. Only when the blue-lightning angel approached him, months after he had passed on, did he realize that he was dead. He became hysterical. Fortunately he recognized the blue-lightning angel because he had learned to call to Archangel Michael earlier in his life. Some people who have passed on don't even recognize an angel when they see one.

This powerful angel took the young man's soul, put him to

---

*The glossary on page 227 defines terms that you may not be familiar with.

sleep, and set him in a heaven-world retreat for those who need to be disassociated from the event of their passing so that they can go on with their soul evolution. There they have a type of rest, even though it's not in the physical body. They may be resting in this retreat for days, hours, weeks, months, or years, depending on the healing process that needs to go on.

That was my last contact with him. He was taken where he needed to be. It was a forward move for him to realize that he was not among the living but among the dead, to go through the process of the shock, and then to be put in a place for the healing of his soul.

Shot by an Intruder

Another example of an afterlife experience is a single woman, a photographer in her late thirties who lived alone. She was shot in her apartment. There was no robbery or sexual abuse, and the motive was unknown.

When I prayed for her, she was on the astral level in the city where she had lived. She was attempting to make her way somewhere but was having a rough time. She was holding on to a railing to keep herself from being swept away by the tides of the darker levels of the afterlife.

I called to the blue-lightning angels to free her. She cried in relief when she saw them coming to rescue her, and she was taken to the heaven-world.

Car Accident

A teenage boy that I knew quite well was killed in a car accident. When I learned of the accident several weeks later, I prayed and called to the angels for him. Various individuals had prayed for him before that, but for whatever reason he was still at the scene of the accident. He could not move, and he could not get away. I don't know why, but for some reason he could not be taken until the time came when I called to the angels.

When the angels came to him, he stood up, recognized them, and asked them to take him where he was supposed to go. They took him to a special retreat in the heaven-world specifically dedicated to teenagers who have gone through a violent or drug-related death. There he joined other teenagers for rehabilitation. Inhabitants of this retreat are assisted in adapting to the shocking experience of suddenly being out of their bodies.

Now that you know there is a place where these people can go to heal, when you hear of teenagers who pass on for these reasons or even those a little older passing on from an unexpected trauma, you can pray fervently to the angels for these people to be taken to this special retreat.

Hemophiliac with AIDS

The next case is a woman who was getting on in years, and she was a hemophiliac. She was a very sweet soul. She had sent me her picture and told me that she was dying of AIDS, which she had received from a blood transfusion. I kept the vigil with her and she eventually passed on.

When I prayed for her after her passing, I discovered that she was already on a certain level of the heaven-world. She was in the body of a little child, running through meadows of grasses and flowers, enjoying herself.

This type of activity, where we can experience the childhood of our souls again, is a healing process and a transition period to prepare the soul to reincarnate and to be delivered of the scars of such a death.

This woman had karma which could only be balanced by her passing in this manner, and the very nature of her passing was just, according to the law of karma. So she was able to pay off a heavy weight of karma, which people often have from past lives, and she will be given the opportunity to reincarnate and to continue working on her soul's evolution.

Protecting the Transition

To be without a physical body can be challenging or even hazardous. The uncertainty involved in this period of transition to the afterlife is why many cultural traditions have prayers for the deceased. Catholics hold wakes with prayers to assist the soul to go to higher realms. The Egyptians had their *Book of the Dead* to guide them through the afterlife. And the *Tibetan Book of the Dead* has prayers that are read to the dead for consecutive days, guiding the one who has left his body to move on and warning him not to fall into dark vibrations.

The stories that I have shared with you may have brought up memories or thoughts of friends, loved ones, or people that you know who have made or may soon make the transition called death. Souls can be taken to their rightful place or even liberated from the astral plane if we call to the angels to descend to those levels and rescue these loved ones.

You may ask, "Why do we have to ask the angels to do this? Don't they do it without our asking them? Why do we need prayer?"

We need prayer because the angels are native to the highest heavenly levels. If they are to descend into our world, they must be called forth by those of us who live here. Angels cannot enter our realm and interfere unless we ask, because we have free will. God has given us free will and dominion over this world. So it's up to us.

Please remember this: We must make calls to the angels for souls who don't have enough wind in their sails to navigate or to get somewhere desirable when they pass away. This is a danger that we all need to be aware of because we can do something about it. We can call to Archangel Michael and his blue-lighting angels and ask them to come to those lower levels and free souls so that they can go to a place of rest and regeneration.

Calling to Archangel Michael

Archangel Michael is the most revered of angels in a number of the world's religious traditions, including Judaism, Christianity, and Islam. I could spend days telling you stories about the intercession of Archangel Michael and his legions of blue-lightning angels in my life and in the lives of people I know. You are no different. Archangel Michael is also your defender. All you have to do is pray or make the call, and he will respond because you are a child of God, a beloved son or daughter of God. The moment you call to heaven, heaven will respond.

Your call can be as simple as this:

Archangel Michael, help me, help me, help me! Archangel Michael, send your blue-lightning angels to free [name of person who has passed on] and take them to heavenly realms.

As you say these words, you send an arc of light from your heart to the heart of this magnificent archangel. When you make that call with fervor, Archangel Michael will instantaneously be at your side. You can visualize him with brilliant blue armour and a sword of blue flame fashioned from pure light substance. He wears a crystalline helmet that is harder than diamond, which shields him against the darkness and shadow of the misqualified energies of the astral plane and our physical world. His aura flashes with the electric blue of God's purity and power.

The more you develop a momentum of calling to Archangel Michael, the more powerfully and swiftly he and his blue-lightning angels will come to your aid and to the aid of those for whom you pray. If you build a momentum and intensity of calling to him, you will establish yourself as a magnet of his energy. He will work through you.

So remember Archangel Michael as you go about your day, both for your own protection and to assist others. This might happen along the highway if you see an accident scene, or when you are watching the news, or anytime you hear about someone's death. It may be loved ones, it may be wrongdoers, or it may be people you don't even know. Archangel Michael and his angels will see to it that they are taken to the level in their afterlife where they need to be.

A Prayer to the Angels

Here is a prayer that you can give for those who are nearing their transition or who have already passed on:

In the name of Almighty God and my own Higher Self,
I call to Archangel Michael and his blue-lightning angels
to free [insert name(s)] and take them safely to a place of
light and healing. I thank you and I accept it done right now.

> *O dearest Michael, archangel of faith,*
> *Around their life protection seal;*
> *Let each new day their faith increase*
> *That God in life is all that's real.*
>
> *Go before them, Michael dear,*
> *Thy shield of faith they do revere;*
> *Armor of light's living flame,*
> *Manifest action in God's name.*
>
> *O Michael, Michael, Prince of Light,*
> *Angel of faith, beautiful, bright:*
> *Around them now protection seal,*
> *Let heaven's faith all error heal.*
>
> *Michael, Michael, raise them now,*
> *To their God Self they will bow;*
> *Scintillating flame of power,*
> *Their vows do keep each blessed hour.*

In full faith I thankfully accept this manifest right here
and now with full power, eternally sustained, and all-
powerfully active!

By establishing a spiritual practice of praying to Archangel Michael, you will be building your relationship with him and his blue-lightning angels to protect your comings and goings, including when you leave your body at the end of this life to move into higher levels of being. And if you determine within your heart that you desire Archangel Michael to come to you at your hour of the transition called death, you can ask him and he will be there for you. And he will help to free you and will assist you to enter into the realms of light with less of the pain that often comes with the fear of passing.

A Prayer for Souls
Who Are Taking Their Leave of the Earth

I offer you another prayer that you can give for departing loved ones, so that you might be comforted in time of bereavement and so that you might comfort others through the intercession of the angels. You can give your personal request for your loved one and then use the prayer given below. I have profound faith that the call is always answered!

Beloved Presence of God in the hearts of all mankind, beloved Archangel Michael and your angelic hosts:

In the name of the souls of humanity—particularly those who shall be called from their mortal forms by our heavenly Father this day—I make this call.

Let the angels of peace stand by the physical body of each soul and hold at perfect peace the aura and feelings of these ones taking their leave of the physical octave and of those present where such release is taking place.

Through the purity of the seraphim of God, let the aura of sanctity be sustained at the solemn hour of transition that the soul may be cut free from her earthly tabernacle by the legions of the archangels.

Let all fear and doubt, sorrow in separation, and grief in the parting of loved ones be consumed by the angels that there be no distress to souls standing at the threshold of a new freedom.

Let the Lord's angels of deliverance meet each soul. Let not a soul belonging to earth's evolution pass through the veil of so-called death unattended.

According to his will, let all children of God who pass from the screen of life this day be taken to heaven-world temples of mercy and forgiveness.

Let them be prepared to pass through their life review in the dignity of their Higher Self and in full conscious awareness, and let each one be assigned to a schoolroom of life and be given the opportunity to study God's law as it pertains to their own evolution.

I call to angels of mercy and love to enfold all those whose loved ones are about to leave or are recently departed this earth, to transmute and consume all burden and sense of loss, and to fill each heart and home with peace and understanding for the opportunity afforded souls called to other realms to progress on the path of eternal life.

So be it! I accept it done in the name of Almighty God, Amen.

CHAPTER 2

What Happens When People Die

*Soon after death occasions the lack of physical senses,
the sight of the world appears to the soul
as if he were seeing it with open eyes when he was living.*

YOGA VASISHTA, ANCIENT HINDU TEXT

A young man collapses on the football field and doesn't get up. He's rushed to the hospital. He has a ruptured spleen, liver, and kidney, and his heart has stopped beating. The doctors try to revive him but fail, and he is pronounced clinically dead.

Meanwhile, this young man is moving out of his body. He feels himself being transported through a dark tunnel toward a bright, white light. Standing in the light is a bearded man who says, "There's more work to be done." Then, seven minutes after he was pronounced dead, the football player suddenly wakes up in the operating room, to the astonishment of doctors and nurses.

You've probably all heard stories about near-death experiences. This real-life story was told to me by one of my students.

The scientific jury is still sifting through evidence on NDEs. Scientists long ago discovered that when they stimulate an area of the brain known as the sylvian fissure, patients report having the sensation of leaving their body and even report seeing long-dead relatives.[1] Thus some modern scientists see the NDE as a defense mechanism of the dying brain. Other researchers dismiss NDEs as wishful thinking or drug-induced hallucinations. However, most of the researchers who have given NDEs serious study do not find these dismissive explanations adequate.

Many NDEs have taken place while patients were brain-dead. Yet later these patients were able to report accurate details about things that happened in the operating room while they were "dead." Melvin Morse, a pediatrician and NDE researcher,* notes that science still can't account for the source of the energy that produces these experiences in someone who is brain-dead. He believes that the area of the sylvian fissure is not the *source* of what someone goes through during an NDE but rather the area of the brain that allows us to *process* mystical experiences. Morse says that this area allows us to tap into a "circuit board of mysticism" that makes us aware of things we can't ordinarily perceive.[2]

Those who have an NDE report that while out of the body they continue to think and feel as they did while in the body, even though in many cases they were brain-dead during the time of the experience. This shows that the brain is not the mind. I want you to think about that. A lot of people think that their brain is their mind. Now, this thought has always seemed very odd to me. If you ever look at a human brain, that certainly isn't what is doing the thinking.

*You can read more about Dr. Melvin Morse's amazing work with children's NDEs in "I Didn't Think You Were Supposed to Be Able to Talk to God" on page 211, Appendix B.

It is your soul that is doing the thinking because your soul is one with the mind of God. The mind of God becomes apparent to you through the brain, through the central nervous system. But you can have awareness anywhere in your body. The brain, then, is the instrument of the mind, and the mind continues on after the brain is dead. Therefore you will not stop thinking or being at the moment someone pronounces you dead. This is a great comfort. You will know everything you've ever known or learned or experienced in this life. It is part of you, and you will take it with you.

I believe that during an NDE the soul leaves the physical body. NDEs confirm what many people already know instinctively: that they are more than their bodies and that they have come and gone from this body and other bodies many times before. NDEs are a valuable experience that God is giving us today to remind us that we are so much more than our bodies. This current life is just one in a long series or chain. People who have had NDEs are typically more likely to believe in reincarnation.

I will share in depth about reincarnation and how essential it is for you to understand it (see chapter 7), but next we will look at some of the experiences and conclusions of those who have had NDEs.

What Happens during an NDE?

The term *near-death experience* was coined by Raymond Moody, a medical doctor with a PhD in philosophy. He has written quite a few books on the subject, including *Life After Life, Reflections on Life After Life,* and *The Light Beyond.* I would like to comment on some of the descriptions that he has gathered during his years of research.

Moody reports that when an NDE begins, the individual may hear himself pronounced dead. He or she may also hear a pleasant or unpleasant ring, buzz, or whooshing sound. I believe that this noise is the sound of the soul disconnecting from the physical body. Feelings of intense pain are replaced by extremely pleasant feelings and sensations. Individuals typically find themselves looking at their own physical body from a point outside of it. They can see the doctors attempting to revive them.

Most subjects report that they found themselves in another body, which Moody dubbed a "spiritual body." They cannot be seen or heard by others in the room. They cannot grip or move physical objects, but they can go through walls. Many subjects have described a floating sensation, a feeling of weightlessness. They find that travel can be instantaneous. People are often at a loss to describe the shape of this body. They may describe it as a cloud of colors or an energy field.

Many subjects report a sensation of being pulled rapidly through a dark space of some kind, often described as a dark tunnel. The dark tunnel represents disconnecting from the physical and entering another plane of consciousness. It's like changing frequencies. At the end of the tunnel they may see a bright light, intense but warm, vibrant, and alive. After they enter the bright light, they meet beings of light and sometimes friends or relatives who have died before them.

Moody writes about other individuals who have had NDEs describing cities of light, libraries, and institutions: "Others describe an entire realm of the afterlife that is set aside for the passionate pursuit of knowledge. One woman described . . . a big university, where people were involved in deep conversations about the world around them. Another man described this realm as a state of consciousness where whatever you want is available to you. If you think of something you want to learn about, it appears to you and is *there for you to learn*."[3]

Some of those who had NDEs saw beautiful pastoral scenes. An elderly man told Moody, "When you get on the other side, there's a river. Just like in *the Bible....* It had a smooth surface, just like glass.... Yeah, you cross a river." When Moody asked how he crossed this river, the man responded, "Just walked.... It's beautiful. There's no way to describe it.... It's so quiet over there and so peaceful. You feel like just resting. There was no darkness."[4]

Seeing friends and relatives and going into pastoral scenes during an NDE may have to do with entering a realm that is entirely subjective, created according to the desires and wishes of the individual. It is known by Buddhists as *devachan.* In devachan you see what you want to see, what you expect to see, and when you want to see it. People may spend decades or centuries (measured as we measure time on earth) in devachan where they are living in a realm of wish fulfillment, playing out their desires and their wishes before they reincarnate. (You will learn more about devachan and other levels of the afterlife in chapter 3.)

Getting on with Moody's analysis of situations that are similar in reports of NDEs, he says, "After meeting several beings of light, the NDEer usually meets a 'supreme Being of Light.' People with a Christian background often describe Him as God or Jesus. Those with other religious backgrounds may call him Buddha or Allah. But some have said that it's neither God nor Jesus, but someone very holy nonetheless."[5]

I believe that the being of light that people see when they go to the other side during an NDE is their Higher Self, which I call the Holy Christ Self—truly the manifestation of the Son of God that is personal to every individual. Moody says that this being radiates such total love and understanding that most people desire to remain with him forever. Your Higher Self is actually with you forever, in every incarnation, and therefore this desire will be satisfied. When you are ready, your soul will be fused to that Self and you will become that Self in action. This is the overarching goal of life.

The Life Review

At the particular moment in time of their near-death experience, individuals cannot stay with this holy one forever. Moody says, "At this point they are told, usually by the Being of Light, that they have to return to their earthly body. But first it's his job to take them on a life review."[6] This being presents to the person "a full color, three-dimensional, panoramic review of every single thing the NDEers have done in their lives."[7] The experience takes place almost instantaneously.

Moody continues, "In this situation, you not only see every action that you have ever done, but you also perceive immediately the effects of every single one of your actions upon the people in your life."[8] This is a review of karma, of causes and effects we have set in motion, of how our actions have affected any or every part of life, and how they will affect us as they come back to us on the return current of life.

He is shown the deeds of his pious and mundane acts, as if they were to continue to eternity. Objects never before seen or thought of also offer themselves to his view. . . .

YOGA VASISHTA, ANCIENT HINDU TEXT

It's true that your Higher Self reviews with you the record of everything that you have done during your life. You can see the ramifications of your actions—how they helped or hurt people. Each action sends out ripples like a pebble dropped into a pond. Your Higher Self does not judge or condemn you during this review. But it is perfectly clear to you where you have succeeded, where you have failed, and what you need to do to make up for your hurtful acts.

Not every soul experiences this life review immediately upon death. Some souls are simply not ready for it. They may be too lost in illusion to accept it, or they may be in shock from the way in which they died. These souls go through a period of sleep or healing before the life review.

Moody writes, "Some people characterize [the life review] as an educational effort on the part of the being of light." This is certainly true. "As they witness the display, the being seems to stress the importance of two things in life: learning to love other people and acquiring knowledge."[9] As I've said over and over again, we will never get to heaven by our doctrine or our dogma. We will only get there by the quality of the love of our hearts.

I think many of us have regrets for the careless or the unkind word, or for the opportunity not taken to give the word of love and peace, and so on. This is the soul's profound desire to balance karma, and it shows the sense of personal accountability that is really native to our souls. But somehow the prevailing winds of the world today say that anything people can get away with is OK.

Lives Turned Around

Some come back from their near-death experience angry at being returned to earth and taken away from the beautiful heaven-world. This anger soon fades as they find greater meaning in life after they return. Moody says, "Many have told me that they felt that their lives were broadened and deepened by their experience, that because of it they became more reflective and more concerned with ultimate philosophical issues. . . . Almost everyone [who had an NDE] has stressed the importance in this life of trying to cultivate love for others, a love of a unique and profound kind."[10] Many also report that they are no longer afraid of death. They do not seek death, but they know that there is life after death.

Often people's lives are turned around by the NDE. For example, Nick was a con artist and criminal who, Moody says, "had done everything from bilking widows to running drugs. . . . He had nice cars, fine clothes, and new houses, and no problems with his conscience to annoy him." Nick was killed by lightning one day while golfing, when a sudden thunderstorm came up. "He met a being of light that he still haltingly describes as God, who graciously led him through a life review." When Nick recovered, he changed his profession. Moody won't say what he does, but he says that it is honest and helpful. "Now," says Nick, "I always live my life knowing that someday I'll have to go through another life review."[11]

Christian teachings tell us that someday there will be a final judgment, when all that we have ever done will be reviewed. But what is left out of this teaching is that each night when we fall asleep, an angel records all of our actions from that day. You may have a review of your record at any time during your life when your soul journeys to a retreat in the heaven-world while your body sleeps at night.

So the life review is there when we need it. These NDEs may be given to people because somehow they are not going to get it any other way. God has great compassion for such people and shows them the impacts of their past actions, thoughts, and feelings, which gives them renewed opportunity.

What's amazing to me about NDEs is the fact that these people actually do die. They are officially pronounced dead. Obviously they must have had very serious conditions in the body, so God provides this experience—and, lo and behold, they come back. Their hearts start beating again, they start breathing again, and they're on their way. There are so many stories now that the NDE appears to be one of the principal ways that the angels are finding to get people on the right track.

Think about the love and mercy of the guardian angels, who are so careful when someone goes through a near-death experience—a terrible accident, lightning, whatever it is. And then the individual gets pulled right back into their body, which starts functioning again. It's miraculous. But the miracle of enlighten-ment through a life review is the greatest miracle—to convince these souls of things that no preacher and no teacher on earth has been able to successfully give them.

What NDEs Can Tell Us

So, what do near-death experiences really mean? First, they show us that we are more than our physical bodies. Many people don't have a problem figuring out that they are more than their physical body, but you would be surprised at just how many people in this world think that they *are* their physical body.

This was always astonishing to me as a child, how someone could think that he was the coat he was wearing. I've always had a sense of myself as a soul occupying this body, being able to come and go at will. I have had the experience of going high up into the atmosphere and watching my body walk down the street and go to work while I was also contemplating other levels of the cosmos.

We have to understand that we are souls who predate these bodies and that we will exist afterwards. The body is a vehicle. We use it until it wears out, just as you get a new car when your old one wears out. And there's nothing more complicated about the story of reincarnation than that. You have more to do than you can do in this life, in this body.

Have you ever felt that you can't get everything done in this lifetime? Well, God agrees with you. That's why he's given you the opportunity for another round and another. And when you get tired of it and want a higher way of life, you'll accelerate on the spiritual path.

Now, not everyone who dies and is resuscitated has an NDE. Some people do and some people don't. Why? You could be chosen for the experience because someone in heaven loves you and wants to tell you that you're on the wrong track, and that if you keep going the way you are going you will wind up in a very bad place. On the other hand, some people have earned their NDE and perhaps need it for their soul evolution. It may remind them that they came to earth to accomplish a certain thing.

We all have a reason for being. If you are not certain what yours is, you need to find out. Whatever else may be our calling or profession in life, I can tell you that our reason for being is to love, to set life free, and to attain reunion with God. How, when, why, where, and with whom you're going to do this remains for you to discover by the gift of free will. Fortunately most of us with some effort can discover our reason for being without having an NDE.

Is the Life Review Enough?

We cannot conclude from the accounts of near-death experiences that we are all going to "a better place." It is important to realize that NDEs do not mean that we are not required to experience the consequences of our actions. There is no sudden change, no miracle transformation, at the moment of transition called death. As you are at the moment of passing, so you are when you behold the other side. You do not suddenly become a saint in heaven if you had no inclination to be one before you died.

Some who have had NDEs may believe that experiencing a life review is atonement enough for past negative deeds. But as my father said to me when I was a tiny child—he looked at me and he said, "It all comes back to you." And he made that remark based on his experience, not because he was a religious man. Would someone be transformed enough merely by seeing and understanding the pain he had caused? Or would he need to experience that pain? An NDE itself does not give enough information about the afterlife to know whether here or hereafter our actions will require atonement.

....

A mere glimpse of Reality may be mistaken
for complete realization.

TIBETAN YOGA AND SECRET DOCTRINES

....

The presence of total love and acceptance emitted by a being of light in an NDE does not prove that there is neither reward nor reparation after the death of the body. What actually happens is that you see instantaneously what is right and wrong. There is no need for judgment on the part of the being of light. At that moment of seeing, of inner knowing, you now have a deep desire to make things right and to get on with the constructive program of undoing the past.

Moody shares that in most NDE cases, "the reward-punishment model of the afterlife is abandoned and disavowed, even by many who had been accustomed to thinking in those terms. They found, much to their amazement, that even when their most apparently awful and sinful deeds were made manifest before the being of light, the being responded not with anger and rage but rather only with understanding and even with humor."[12]

Would a loving and understanding God require atonement of a soul? Isn't forgiveness instantaneous, even before we ask? The reality is that although there is no condemnation, we *are* required to balance our debts to every part of life, and then we can move on. After the transition called death, when you go through a life review, it will be apparent to you what your karma is, what obligations you must fulfill on earth before you can graduate from earth's schoolroom. If you have unfinished business and lessons to learn, you may need to return to earth for another incarnation after a stay in an etheric retreat. The term *etheric* encompasses the many realms of the heaven-world, which I will describe more fully later on. In cities of light and spiritual retreats at etheric levels, you can learn lessons to prepare you for your next round on earth. Yes, you will then reincarnate.

So there is no need for condemnation. These beings of light never engage in condemnation, anger, or rage. They deal with your karmic reality. And reality is what it is. Karma gives back to you exactly what you sent forth. There is no greater love expressed in the universe than through God's law of karma. Being on the receiving end of the causes we have set in motion teaches us the law of the circle and the consequences of our own actions and inactions to every part of life. Karma teaches us to love and to love and to love, as no other process can or does. You cannot feel the pain you have inflicted on someone else unless that pain is experienced by you. You cannot develop compassion, remorse, pity, humility, mercy, and sensitivity to life if you do not have the law of karma to teach you.

The law of karma is actually the law of love, teaching us to do unto others as we would have them do unto us. Karma is for the development of the soul. It teaches us to pay our debts. It is *because* God loves us that he allows our karma to return to us. We created it, and we have to uncreate it. Only thus can we fulfill our reason for being as co-creators with our Father-Mother God.

Breaking the Rules

Some people ask, "If the afterlife is so beautiful, why shouldn't we just commit suicide so we can go there?" Dr. Moody found that those who had had near-death experiences after committing suicide described an unpleasant experience. The conflicts they had attempted to escape were still present. Moody writes about a man who shot himself because he was depressed about the death of his wife. The man died but was resuscitated. He later reported to Moody, "I didn't go where [my wife] was. I went to an awful place. . . . I immediately saw the mistake I had made. . . . I thought, 'I wish I hadn't done it.'" Moody says that he is not making a moral judgment but writes that NDEers who attempted suicide and experienced an unpleasant place feel that "This was their penalty for 'breaking the rules' by trying to release themselves prematurely from what was, in effect, an 'assignment'— to fulfill a certain purpose in life."[13]

I can tell you that in 99 percent of the cases, those who attempt to follow loved ones in death by suicide do not go where their loved ones are. This is the illusion of the demons of suicide, who taunt people to get them to exit life before they have fulfilled their reason for being. We need to be extremely vigilant if we become aware of people who may be suicidal. We must also be vigilant concerning very aggressive thought projections, what I refer to as aggressive mental suggestion. This can bombard the mind when it is weak or burdened, preying upon the mind to convince someone to take their own life.

So what happens when someone dies by suicide? As long as the person has good credits of karma, he will come right back into incarnation so that he can never feel that suicide is an escape of responsibility or unpleasant situations. The karmic result of suicide may be immediately entering a new body as an infant and being sent right back to a similar set of difficult circumstances in order to face them again. That's *if* the soul merits an immediate new opportunity to incarnate.

Moody says that one young man who attempted suicide found himself in a place resembling hell. Others who had attempted suicide reported that they felt they would have stayed in an unpleasant place for quite a while if they had not returned to their bodies. People who have died by suicide and who have not accumulated good karma may find themselves in a place of great darkness, an unpleasant limbo state. When people have not garnered enough light by serving life in some way, or have not led good lives in this life or past lives, they cannot get out of these realms of darkness without help.

I've devoted many hours to praying and calling to the angels to rescue departed souls. You can also learn to make calls so that family and friends can get to a better place in the afterlife. Angels will rescue them, but departed souls need to be aware that angels are good beings who are coming to help them. Then they will not deny the angels when they arrive.

Caught in the Lower Realms

The existence of these unpleasant places that some people saw in NDEs as they traveled to the spiritual realms shows that there are places other than the realms of light where people go when they die. One woman described to Moody a place that he named "a realm of bewildered spirits." This realm is somewhere in the astral plane, one of those lower levels on the descending scale. (You will learn more about these levels in chapter 3.)

During Moody's interview with this woman, she reported that the bewildered people "seemed to be forever shuffling and moving around, not knowing where they were going, not knowing who to follow or what to look for. . . . They would start straight, then veer to the left and take a few steps and veer back to the right. And absolutely nothing to do. Searching, but for what . . . I don't know."[14] This is the description of a ship without a rudder or a captain or a compass. Someone who is without the love of the will of God will have no direction in this life or in the next. Only when we are one-pointed toward our God Presence will we attain our short- and long-term goals.

This woman also shared that these spirits are "very bewildered; not knowing who they are or what they are. It looks like they have lost any knowledge of who they are, what they are— no identity whatsoever."[15] If you allow yourself to get into this directionless state, you may not get out of it for generations or centuries, as earthly time is counted.

The discarnates (those who have passed on, no longer have a physical body, and remain in the lower levels near the physical earth) reminded this woman of "what I have read of as descriptions of ghosts; they would be mainly the see-through type of thing. There seems to have been a great huge array of them around."[16] These beings cannot communicate with those on earth, though they try. One of these beings was trying to talk to young children and to an older woman who were all living in the same house. This being was "trying to get them to do the right things, to change so as not to be left like she was. 'Don't do as I did, so this won't happen to you. Do things for others so that you won't be left like this.'. . . It seemed that in this house there was no love. . . . It seemed that she was trying to atone for something she had done."[17]

Several other NDEers who had seen confused spirits in similar states of existence agreed on a number of points in their interviews with Moody: The bewildered spirits appeared to be stuck because they were "unable to surrender their attachments to the physical world. . . . They seemed bound to some particular object, person, or habit. . . . These beings appeared 'dulled,'. . . Their consciousness seemed somehow limited. . . ." These souls would remain there until they solved the problems of non-resolution that were holding them there.[18] In these cases, Moody was interviewing people who had witnessed the astral plane during their NDEs.

I've seen many souls who have had burdens at the deepest level of their beings, even unconscious levels. They had never really made their peace with God. Until you do that, life is surely a struggle. We war within ourselves, between the lower self and the Higher Self.

The Spiritual Equation

The bewildered spirits are those in whom the divine spark that God has given to each one of us has gone out. They may have spent many, many lifetimes paying no attention to God whatsoever. We all start out equal. We were all given an equal quantity of light. But somewhere along the way these bewildered souls squandered that light, so they have no inner direction that points them. It is a most tragic state.

The descriptions of what happens after suicide and of people trapped in the "realm of bewildered spirits" reaffirm the principle of karma. These examples show us that there is a cause-and-effect relationship between our deeds in life and our destination after death. We will all be assigned to one of the levels of either the astral plane or the etheric plane when we pass from our life on earth—unless we have such attainment that we reunite with God in the ritual of the ascension immediately at the conclusion of this life. But we can do much while we are still on earth to up our grade and improve our future. This is the great key I want you to have and use.

So it is through other people's eyes and experiences, possibly even people we know who have had near-death experiences, that we know a little bit more about life and death and the transition to etheric realms. But there is much more to be aware of.

Before I give you more detail about these heavenly or etheric levels and the astral levels—what they are for and why souls gravitate to them—I want to share with you an excerpt of a radio interview that I did with a woman who attempted suicide and came back with a new perspective on life after her near-death experience.

....

A single glimpse of heaven is enough to confirm its existence, even if it is never experienced again.
It is my strong suspicion that even one such experience might be able to prevent suicide, . . .
and perhaps many varieties of slow self-destruction.

ABRAHAM MASLOW, AMERICAN PSYCHOLOGIST

....

To the Edge of Hell and Back

Interview by Elizabeth Clare Prophet with Angie Fenimore,[19] author of *Beyond the Darkness.*

Elizabeth Clare Prophet: Today we're going to explore one woman's account of her amazing near-death experience. We've all heard stories of those who have passed beyond the veil and come back to tell us what heaven is like. But today our guest is Angie Fenimore, whose near-death experience took her to the edge of hell and back again.

ECP: Miraculously you were restored to life, and I am certain that many, many people have benefited from that miracle in your life. So please tell us about it.

Angie: I'd had just a really tragic childhood—a lot of horrible things that happened to me that I kind of just stuffed. I didn't really deal with them at all. And it wasn't until I was married and had a couple of children that memories started resurfacing, and I struggled with that. I went to a support group for survivors of sexual abuse, which was just one of the many things that happened to me. . . .

And for me, hearing the stories of other survivors made my pain actually deeper. I felt like my problems were different from the other women that I spoke with. I really started to turn inward and just cut myself off from other people and kind of lived a separate reality. I'd still go grocery shopping and see my friends, but they had no idea what was going on inside of me. I don't think anybody really did, even my husband.

I just came to a point where I felt like I couldn't overcome this. I just couldn't, and I was terrified that I was going to pass these horrible traits on to my children, that they were going to suffer from the same kind of depression that I suffered from and that they were all better off without me.

It was January, and I had gone to the grocery store, just kind of like a little convenience store. We lived in Okinawa, Japan, at the time, and this was just a little shop on base, and I didn't even bother to change out of my sweats. I went in in my slippers and grabbed the milk and I went home. I pulled into the parking space but I could not make myself go in the house. I just couldn't do it.

So I just left. I pulled out and I left and found a place to hole up for the night. And the next day I went to a movie, went shopping and got myself some shoes and some clothing and washed my hair in the sink in the bathroom. I didn't call home. I didn't let anybody know where I was. I just felt this terrible, deep need to escape, and it would not go away no matter what I did.

When I finally went home, I was devastated by what I'd put my family through. I couldn't believe that I was capable of hurting them that deeply. And I think it was later that night when everybody else went to sleep, that I decided that I just wasn't going to put them through it anymore. I slit my wrists and took a bottle of pills, which came back up. And so I went and dug through my medicine cabinet and took everything that was in there, kind of slowly—just kept taking it so it wouldn't come back up, and sent my kids off to a neighbor when it was a decent hour. And that was when it happened.

ECP: That must have been a most profound turning point in your life, reaching the depths of hell and then climbing back up again and living to tell the tale so that of all of us can also understand that if we follow this route, we may not have the saving that you had.

AF: What happened to me was I had had a stepmother who had had a near-death experience and shared it with me. But it was before anybody had even talked about near-death experiences, so I wasn't sure whether even to believe her. But it happened when I was very young, before she knew me. I was probably fourteen when she told me about it.

And what she had told me was that she went up to the corner of the room (she had been in a car accident) and that she was greeted by beings of light who told her she wasn't done, that she still had a mission here. But she was given a choice. So that's what I expected when I laid down on the couch. I felt this intense power—very, very powerful energy, stronger than I can even describe really—and I couldn't tell whether it was in the room or just within me.

ECP: What's the first thing that happened to you after you went out of your body? How did it make you feel?

AF: Well, because of what my stepmother told me, I was expecting to see myself down on the couch from up in the corner of the room. And so I opened my eyes as I felt this energy pull me out of my body. I knew I'd left my body. But when I opened my eyes, I was pulled back in. This happened to me a few times. And then I realized that I had to exercise my own will to make this happen, that it wasn't a natural thing and I was going to have to force it. So I just really concentrated very hard and that's when it happened.

The first thing that happened to me was I went directly into my life review, and it started with my birth. And I experienced my birth, but it was from everybody's perspective—my mother's, everybody's. And that was probably the most interesting thing for me because I remembered things entirely differently as an adult than they had actually unfolded for me in my life. I was shown that my parents loved me, that they struggled like everybody struggles and made mistakes like everybody does.

When my life review was over—and I felt a presence with me; there was somebody there with me that I couldn't see and—but I swung my head around to look and I was surrounded by this darkness. It was a thick, foreboding entity. It wasn't just an absence of light. This had a very powerful energy about it. As I looked around, I saw a line of teenagers standing next to me. As I leaned over and looked at them, I thought to myself, "Oh, my gosh, we're the suicides." I could see in their faces that they were just dead in every sense of the word. There was no hope, no life or energy. And from the way they were dressed, I could tell that they listened to the same kind of music that I listened to, this very dark kind of music, alternative kind of stuff.

Co-host: In your book you say that music plays a very important role in your attempted suicide and the suicides of others. How important is music really?

AF: Well, I had been told and had believed up until this experience that we're inspired by what the music is telling us. But my experience told me (because not everybody who listens to the same kind of music I did at the time is going to commit suicide) that's not what happens.

What happens is that everything has a spiritual creation before it has a physical creation, everything including music. And we all have within us a measure of darkness or of light and this is constantly changing. And music is a very, very powerful tool in altering that balance within us and within the space that we inhabit. We just can't see this darkness and light always, even though when I came back I could see it in people. But if I'm not always in tune and doing everything I know I need to be doing, then that leaves me as well. It's not a given thing.

But anyway, what happens when this music inspired by God is played, the energy changes and light comes into that area, into that space. And probably the very spirits who inspired it, or even just spirits of light, will be there. And that is what happens when music of darkness is played as well. It is inspired by darkness. When we play music, these spirits gather. It's an invitation.

ECP: You had a turning point where you saw a single pinpoint of light. Tell us about that.

AF: After I saw the teenagers, I was taken to a different place. There were so many people that were filled with darkness. I looked around at them and realized that I heard a voice that these other people didn't hear. I turned to look where this voice was coming from. An incredible power accompanied it, and I could feel the energy around me was saying, "This is God, this is God."

They were worshiping him, these little particles of energy. As he spoke I could see where he was coming from. It looked like a single star out there. He said, "Is this what you really want?" And he came toward me with incredible speed but stopped some distance from where I was. Where I was, was very dark. I could tell that he couldn't come into this place. I didn't know whether it was that he wouldn't or that he couldn't.

I was in awe. I couldn't believe it but I knew that this was God. And it was incredible, this feeling of love that I had from him. It was like I was his daughter. I had never felt or understood that in my life, even with all of the religious experiences I had had. I had gone to many, many churches and I felt that I was different from everybody else. They felt at home there, and I was just the adopted daughter. . . .

What I felt from him was an all-encompassing, all-knowing kind of love. It wasn't that he loved me for what I had done that was right or good—it was that he loved me in spite of everything. And he knew everything.

Co-host: Angie, many people think that their lives don't count, that they're really not important people. One of the things that I think that you were trying to say in your book was that everybody's life does count and that you influence many, many other people.

AF: Every little decision we make has tremendous impact. We affect everybody in our circle and those people in turn affect people in their circles and those people in turn affect other people. In that way we pass this light or this dark energy, whichever it is we choose to pass on, which is why it's so important to correct those things we do that are mean or thoughtless.

CHAPTER 3

What Are Your Afterlife Options?

*If there are no dogs in Heaven, then when I die
I want to go where they went.*

WILL ROGERS

The choices you make, which often become a matter of habit over the course of your life, determine where you go after you leave your body at the time of your passing. Your decisions day by day can and will impact not only where you go when you leave your body during sleep at night but where you will find yourself in the afterlife. I encourage you to be aware of what you are doing during your journey through life and of the nature of cause and effect.

I want to tell you a story to illustrate how what you might think were trivial choices affected someone's afterlife. I had someone who was working for me, a very precious woman. She passed on suddenly in an accident. I had not known before, but I learned from her daughter what this woman's secret weakness was. Her daughter told me what a wonderful mother she was, and she was indeed. But she also told me how she and her mother would spend hours together over the years watching old movies with the old songs and the old music, playing them again and again.

Her mother had put so much energy into watching these old movies that she had enmeshed herself in the astral plane with the desires that were portrayed in them—to have many admirers, to fall in love, and to live happily ever after. The mother actually entered into her devachan (the lower levels of the heaven-world where one experiences wish fulfillment of one's good karma after passing on), while she was still in physical incarnation, when she could have been working to free herself from these habit patterns.

This sweet soul had had great difficulties and sorrow in her life in terms of marriage and children. She was longing for the fulfillment of her dreams to such an extent that she had saturated herself with the old films and music, and she was very attached to the music.

You may have seen on TV where certain ads bring back songs from decades ago. People who are in their fifties and sixties, who lived in those eras, are shown on the ads as saying how great it is to sit and hear all the old songs, to think about all their old friends and what they used to do when they were teenagers, and to relive the whole experience. When these ads start playing old songs, listeners instantaneously remember when and where and what they were doing, and with whom. This reminiscing becomes almost more dangerous than obvious evil because of the subtlety of its effect.

Some people don't want to live in reality. They create their little world of illusion that insulates them from the challenges of karma and from what they must be up and doing in this life. Having built an unreal world around themselves, they don't tune in to current issues. They don't give a second thought to politics or to crisis on an international scale. They are anesthetized by what they are eating, by what they are taking in through TV, and by what they're taking in through music.

Unfortunately, these people are so saturated in delusion by the time they pass on that instead of going to the real devachan at heavenly levels, they find themselves in the astral plane. And there is so little difference between the life they have lived on earth and their life in the astral plane that they scarcely know that their transition has taken place. So these seemingly insignificant little choices can easily become a downward spiral.

The conclusion of this story is that the mother did go into the astral plane and spend some time there after she passed on. And I could not, with all my prayers, get her released. She was living out her illusions and all the fantasies of the movies she had seen. She was partying every night and had male admirers surrounding her everywhere. Now this doesn't mean that she did not eventually move on, but there's no sense in stepping into a mud puddle if it can be avoided! Time spent on earthly distractions is time that could have been spent balancing karma. And time spent in the astral plane is time that could have been spent making real spiritual progress.

Unfortunately, there are many who do not reach the heaven-world between incarnations. They live on the other side as they do in this world, without higher aspirations and caught up in material desires. They reincarnate from these levels, having risen no higher than the astral plane, and thus they have no recollection of anything but a meager, puny existence.

Desire Propels All Levels of Being

Lesser desires can propel you to a lower level of existence in the afterlife, where you may not even have karma. Unfulfilled desires bring us back into physical incarnation and take us to the place where we can fulfill those desires. If we cannot surrender a desire, we will still have the longing for it until the desire is fulfilled. The quickest way to move on is to fulfill the desire. Get it over with and see it for what it is. Then we can hope to not have to go through the same thing ten thousand times in order to learn from a set of experiences that there is a certain futility in the fulfillment of all the human desires we have.

Some desires, on the other hand, are divinely ordained. We can enjoy life and be happy on the spiritual path, with companionship and fulfillment, education, profession, children, happy families, and so forth. Desires become inordinate desires only when they become more important to us than our spiritual path. It's a delicate balance.

As I've said, the choices you make in this lifetime and those you have made in previous lifetimes determine what level you will be assigned to when your soul makes the transition called death. If you haven't finished what you came to do down here, you may not get to the best place. In order to get to the higher levels of light, you must have developed a spiritual momentum of the sacred fire of the heart. The way to do this is to focus on giving love—not just human love but divine love, a spiritual love, and a compassion that both meets the human need and transcends it.

The bewildered spirits described in Raymond Moody's book, those who were observed wandering around on the astral plane as ghosts, were there for two reasons: First, they never developed the divine spark that God gave them. They simply lived their lives for pleasure and for their own selfish pursuits. They did not increase their heart flame. And so when they got to the other side, they had no sacred fire in them to propel them to higher octaves. Second, they were still attached to the pleasures of the flesh. They were the victims of their desires.

Desire propels all levels of being. Your heart is where your desires are; your desires are where your heart is. And this determines where you will be, here in this life and in the hereafter. You are the product of your desires, which propel you like the outboard motor in a motorboat. If you desire to keep on experiencing human life but in a higher form, you need to balance your karma on earth so that you have the option to live in the golden etheric cities of light instead of on the physical level of this earth. A little suffering, much self-discipline, much determination, doing what you have to do (like it or not), will give you tremendous options in the eternity to come.

The Flytrap of Life on Earth

Even though there are many exciting things to look forward to in the future, such as advances in technology and space exploration, you need to remember that experiments in physicality can literally go on forever. You can will yourself to reincarnate, returning to physical life forever and forever. But as long as you are locked in to the physical plane, you have locked-in limitation, locked-in mortality, and locked-in potential for tragedy as well as triumph. You have built-in obsolescence.

You don't have to keep coming back here in order to enjoy the experiences in life. The physical plane is a flytrap. Once you get into it, you can't get out of it because the more you're in it, the more you like it, and the more you desire to be part of it.

And then desire endows the world of illusion with a greater and greater reality. These unfulfilled desires can be very troublesome. They burden the psyche and can create very deep psychological problems in all of us.

Now, because of your attachment to life on earth, you're locked in to karma and karma-making desire. And karma begets karmic density, rendering dull the senses and the mind and creating the poison of self-ignorance—not knowing who you are and the ultimate goal of life. The karma of ignorance begets more ignorance, and then you can no longer find your way back to the shining city of light in the etheric realms of the heaven-world.

Many Cultures, Many Mansions

There are as many heavens and hells as there are people. Jesus told us that there are many mansions in his Father's house. Saint Paul speaks of the third heaven. But the idea that there is more to the afterlife than one heaven and one hell (and possibly a purgatory) has roots in a number of spiritual traditions of East and West.

I knew a man in Christ above fourteen years ago,
(whether in the body, I cannot tell;
or whether out of the body, I cannot tell: God knoweth;)
such an one caught up to the third heaven.

SAINT PAUL, KJV

Jewish mystics believe that there are seven or more heavens. The Jewish mystical system called the Kabbalah tells us that we create our own heaven or hell. And the Jewish mystical text the Zohar tells us that there are many abodes in heaven, with gradations of glory and splendor, even as the works of the righteous vary.

....

And I measured out the whole earth, its mountains,
and all hills, fields, trees, stones, rivers, all existing things
I wrote down, the height from earth to the seventh heaven,
and downwards to the very lowest hell, and the
judgment-place, and the very great, open and weeping hell.

ENOCH

....

Students of Neoplatonism in the second and third centuries believed that there were many levels of reward and punishment in the afterlife. Hindu and Buddhist texts also describe different heavens. One common Hindu description gives seven levels of heaven and seven levels of hell. A Buddhist conception is that there are twenty-eight heavens. The bottom twenty-four are known as the heavens of form, where people experience joy and happiness but are still tied to the material world. The four highest are known as the heavens of the formless world. They are at the point where Matter and Spirit meet.

Octaves and Dimensions of the Afterlife

The spiritual traditions concerning the afterlife around the world and through the ages are fascinating and demonstrate that the afterlife having many levels is not a new idea. But how can we understand and influence where we find ourselves among these many levels? The chart on the following page is your road map to visualize where you are going in this life and the next.

I sometimes call the different levels of the afterlife *octaves.* These octaves are going up the scale, accelerating upward, or they are descending to lower notes, like the notes in a musical scale. In music, sound waves go up in frequency as you go up the scale. But if you jump up an entire octave, you will find that you can re-create at a higher level the same notes that you played in the lower octave—do, re, mi, and so on. The notes are simply at a higher frequency.

So, too, there are octaves of light that operate at higher energy levels than the frequency we know as Matter. We can think of these octaves as planes of existence that vibrate at different frequencies of energy. In order to reach these octaves of light, we simply need to raise the frequency at which we energetically vibrate—something we will be discussing later. There are also octaves that operate at lower frequencies than Matter.

33 LEVELS ABOVE AND BELOW	
The Etheric, Physical, and Astral Planes	
REALM OF SPIRIT (Nirvana of formlessness)	
ETHERIC PLANE (Heaven-world)	
31–33	Nirvana of form
18	Level from which the ascended masters' teachings are given
12	Tushita heaven, the Pure Land of Maitreya
7	Level of life on Venus
1–3	Devachan, realm of wish-fulfillment
PHYSICAL PLANE The Crossroads	You can integrate with the etheric or astral while here.
ASTRAL PLANE (Lower levels of the afterlife)	
1–7	Realm of illusion
8–32	Beginning of what we would call hell, increasing in darkness to the 33rd level
33	Absolute Evil and Darkness

None of these octaves are up in the sky or down under the ground, as people used to quaintly think in the past. Since we know that atoms and molecules are made up of mostly empty space, other octaves may exist in the same space that we are occupying right now. We cannot perceive them, and they cannot perceive us. Today, physicists are postulating other dimensions and parallel universes. When we unlock the secrets of these, we may have also unlocked the secrets of heaven and hell.

There are thirty-three levels of the heaven-world in an ascending scale, which I call the *etheric octave*. And there are thirty-three levels of the astral plane in a descending scale. Let's take a closer look at these levels of the afterlife.

A World of Infractions and Delusions

The frequency of the astral plane is a lower vibrating level than the physical plane. It is the repository of the collective thought and feeling patterns, conscious and unconscious, of humanity. Although the real purpose of the astral plane is to amplify the pure thoughts and feelings of God in us, it has instead become polluted with all of our negative feelings, emotions, and desires.

Thus the astral plane is a world of illusion where things are not really what they seem. Souls who have passed on can easily become trapped there, and then they may not be able to find a way out. It's the world where all of your bad dreams come true and you can't wake up.

The upper levels of the astral plane are not that different from some places on the physical earth. They are levels where people go who may be nice people but who basically live selfish lives and do not contribute much to their families or communities. In these levels, you often find people sitting around gossiping, playing cards, just being spiritually stagnant.

So the first level of the astral plane is a plane of illusion and delusion and of souls who have been inclined to certain infractions of life that are not so serious. One can get out of these planes more easily. You can think of levels one to seven as limbo or purgatory. But going down from the first levels of the astral plane, you find levels where there is a heavier karma and where the individual did not acquire enough light to get to even the very first heaven-world. There was perhaps no centering in the Higher Self, no acknowledgment of a Supreme Being, no sense of service by loving one another.

Getting to the heaven-world really doesn't have to do with what your religious doctrine is. You could belong to any religion or none. What it has to do with is how much you have loved. One never gets to heaven by doctrine. One gets to heaven by the expression of love toward life that is a pure love—a love that is not controlling, not deceptive, but simply desires to help others achieve their oneness with God.

People in and out of religion are found in the astral realms, and it has to do with what their deeds have been. The physical world is all about deeds. We can think good thoughts all day, and that's helpful. But we have to get out there in the arena of action.

If someone gets too deep into the astral plane, perhaps through drugs or through other things that impact the mind and the body, it's difficult for that person to get out unless someone on earth calls to Archangel Michael to descend into the astral plane and rescue that soul. Let's say that "too deep" is below the eighth level. You don't have to get very far into the astral plane before it can feel like you're hiking somewhere and suddenly your right leg goes into a deep hole or crevasse and you fall in. We can't learn and grow in the astral plane. It's where we may even be subject to the manipulations and attacks of souls who have chosen to merge with their lower nature.

The Lower Realms of Hell

There are places in the afterlife that are as bad or even worse than some of the worst places on earth. Beginning at level eight, the astral plane takes on the characteristics of what we would call hell. As one goes deeper and deeper and deeper into the depths of the astral plane, the various levels are compartments of those who have more and more serious karma, until you are in the realms of death and hell itself. This is where you find souls who have spent their lives consciously abusing others, misusing power, and so forth.

The bottom level is the thirty-third level. It takes going down that many levels to get to the place of absolute Evil. Those in the very lowest levels of darkness are those who have been responsible for hundreds, thousands, or even millions of deaths and for much suffering and pain.

Take note that these individuals have not been destroyed, even though they have committed crimes against humanity. But this is where souls are who have done such destruction on earth that it is questionable whether they will reincarnate at all. Life requires, as the expiation of their karma, that these souls experience the pain that they have inflicted upon others. In a sense, by being in that lowest level of the astral plane they are working through their karma.

The Beginning of Heaven

Now that you have an idea about the astral realms from top to bottom, I would like to tell you more about devachan, which I introduced earlier during our discussion of near-death experiences. I think of devachan as the bottom three levels of the etheric octaves. *Devachan* is a Buddhist term meaning "dwelling place of the shining one." In Buddhism, it is the subjective heaven-state in which one lives between earth lives after the death of the physical body.

At the point that your soul makes the transition, you go to the inner level for which you have fitted yourself during your life. After your life review, you may be assigned to a level of devachan. In the lowest levels of the etheric octave, there is actually a kind of kindergarten for souls. Here they learn the ABCs of cosmic law that their teachers on earth have not taught them.

Devachan is a realm where you may experience your desires that were unfulfilled during your life on earth. This does not include sensual desires. The sensual desires of your lower nature are left at the door, so to speak, of the etheric octave. Devachan is a place where your bad karma is set aside. You are allowed to simply sit back and experience your good karma or to learn things that will prepare you for your next life.

In *The Mahatma Letters,* the Master K.H. says that devachan is *"a state . . .* of *intense selfishness* [meaning dealing with the self], during which an *Ego* reaps the reward of his *unselfishness* on earth [meaning receiving the rewards that are due to that self]."[1] But if you have the good karma to experience such a reward, you may in many cases decide not to experience it. You have the choice to go on to even higher octaves if you do not want to spend your time in the lower etheric octaves of devachan. The lower devachan is where souls go who are not ready for instruction in the higher octaves.

If people are in a high state of consciousness when they die, they do not have to go to devachan after death. Instead, they may go directly to places of spiritual learning. They may study under advanced souls known as ascended masters, who are the saints and sages of East and West, now graduated from earth's schoolrooms, who offer to be guides and teachers on our spiritual path. (You will learn more about these masters and their retreats a bit later.) Although devachan is seen by Buddhists as a place where people experience the rewards of good deeds on earth, devachan is not the ultimate goal. The goal is to reach the nirvana of formlessness, which is beyond devachan and at a higher frequency than the heavenly paradises of the etheric plane.

The Higher Heaven-Worlds

The heaven-world is quite organized. After you study in the schoolroom of the first level of the etheric plane, you graduate to the next and the next, if you choose to apply yourself. Then you progress higher and higher and higher. Finally, the thirty-third plane is the highest octave of the heaven-world before the nirvana of formlessness.

Life on Venus is at the seventh etheric level, where the evolutions have attained to a greater light and a greater beauty than we have attained on Earth. Life on Venus cannot be perceived by those of us who are on Earth because it is in another dimension or wavelength. It is seven steps up into the etheric from the physical octave as we know it.

There are cities of light in etheric octaves. They are congruent with earth, but we do not tune in to them because of our lower vibration. In these cities are all the splendid things that anyone could dream of for a golden age. In the higher octaves there is still form and experience, culture and civilization, homes and families. But life in higher octaves is in a more ideal state than life on earth, and people are not in the physical plane. They are embodying the precepts of love and the laws of God and elements of their Higher Self.

The Buddhist Tushita heaven, or "pure land," is at the twelfth level of the etheric octave. This is where Maitreya Buddha and his disciples, the bodhisattvas, abide. Each level is increasing in light and vibration. A soul cannot go from one level to the next without having passed certain initiations and tests.

Block print image of Buddha's descent from Tushita heaven

According to the teachings of Mahayana Buddhism, a pure land, or buddha-field, is a spiritual realm or paradise presided over by a Buddha. A pure land is first conceived when a bodhi-sattva, out of compassion for sentient beings, makes a vow that after he has attained supreme Buddhahood he will establish a pure land where conditions will be ideally suited to the attainment of greater enlightenment. Therefore a bodhisattva is willing to forgo the bliss of nirvana to save those who have not attained enlightenment. The pure lands are described in Buddhist writings as beautiful abodes, rich and fertile, inhabited by gods and men. They are devoid of all pain or sin as well as the problems of everyday existence.

There are other paradises at etheric levels presided over by different Buddhas. Here is an excerpt from a sutra, or scripture, describing another Buddha's pure land: "In that world Sukhavati, O Sariputra, there is neither bodily nor mental pain for living beings. The sources of happiness are innumerable there. For that reason is that world called Sukhavati (the happy)....
That world ... is adorned with seven terraces, with seven rows of palm trees, and with strings of bells. It is enclosed on every side, beautiful, brilliant with the four gems, viz. gold, silver, beryl and crystal. With such arrays of excellencies peculiar to a Buddha country is that Buddha country adorned."[2]

In *A Survey of Buddhism,* Buddhist monk and scholar Sangharakshita explains that this paradise may be "thought of as a kind of cosmic Sangha [community], unthinkably vaster and infinitely more perfect than the institution which is as it were its shadow here on earth. One who comes into being in this spiritual kingdom is free from the evil destinies; he has no more to fear rebirth as ... a tormented being. Problems of food, clothing and means of livelihood perplex him not. His whole concern is with the attainment of Enlightenment."[3]

Moving upward, for people to go to the eighteenth level after making the transition called death, they have to have a lot of attainment. The eighteenth level is the level from which I receive teachings from the ascended masters and other beings of light. This level is necessary for the accuracy of the teachings they give us. This doesn't mean that I am always at the eighteenth level, but I am there when I am receiving teachings from the masters. This is the level in which these beings abide who give their teachings to benefit souls of light on earth.

Nirvanas of Form and Formlessness

As you go from the nineteenth to the thirty-third level, you are approaching the nirvana of formlessness. The highest levels of the etheric plane are called the nirvana of form. There is a nirvana where you retain your form and there is a nirvana that is without form. Beyond the thirty-third level of the heaven-world is the nirvana of formlessness.

If you were to go from level to level, I think you would see yourself going from world to world. There's a blending. As you go higher in consciousness and in thought, you merge with higher levels. And if you are leading a spiritual life and you have a daily practice of communion with God—of prayers, of mantras, of meditation—you are passing through these levels to higher and higher states as you balance your karma.

Karma is the greatest detractor from being able to go higher in the afterworld. You have to be lighter, as if you were going up in a balloon. You can't have a lot of ballast. These are the gradations of your soul moving upward. The idea is to always be ahead of the game and to always know that if God calls your soul Home today or tomorrow, you have accomplished what you were supposed to do on earth and you can move on in the cycles of being.

If you achieve that tenth or twentieth octave, you are in a very high place. You are able to accelerate in etheric retreats and cities with cosmic beings, with Buddhas. You can spend time in that etheric octave. Then you can come back and be a great leader or teacher, if this is what you want to do. You can reincarnate from the etheric plane.

The souls must reenter the absolute substance
whence they have emerged. But to accomplish this,
they must develop all the perfections, the germ of which is
planted in them; and if they have not fulfilled this condition
during one life, they must commence another,
a third, and so forth, until they have acquired the
condition which fits them for reunion with God.

THE ZOHAR, A KABBALAH TEXT

I'll say it again: What determines where you go when you make the transition called death is your state of consciousness and your actions during your life. You set the sail! Remember that. As you come to the end of this life, remember that you have to be the captain of your ship and set your sail for where you want to go and what you want to be. Don't let somebody else do it for you. You need to know where you're going, and you have to determine this with your guardian angel and with the legions of light.

The Soul's Vehicles

Now I am going to discuss in more detail the process by which the soul enters devachan. First, let's define the vehicles of the soul. You have four interpenetrating vehicles of consciousness, which I often refer to as the four lower bodies. You have the physical body, which of course you can see. The other three bodies are larger bodies that you cannot see.

In addition to the physical body, you have an emotional

body (sometimes called the desire body or astral body), which can be very large. Our feelings extend from ourselves tremendously and influence every part of life. If we qualify energy in a positive way, our feelings of love can be felt throughout a city and across the world. The desire body is the body that is often most out of control.

Next you have your mental body, which is the vehicle for your mind. Your thinking mind is an envelope that surrounds and interpenetrates the physical body. But your mind is really an extension of infinite intelligence. We all plug in to the same "central computer" of the mind of God, and we all have our "computer stations" in our brains. And we have access to the knowledge that we need and want.

You also have an etheric body, the highest vibrating body of the four. The etheric body, (also called the body of memory), contains all the records of this life and all previous lives—your stream of identity. It carries the blueprint of your life—the image and likeness of God in which you were made. But it also carries the lower images that you have created about yourself—images of limitation.

These four lower bodies are interpenetrating sheaths of consciousness. They function as one unit. We can think, remember, feel, and have physical sensations all at once. We are entirely integrated, although some of us are more centered in the physical, others more in the emotional or mental, and yet others more in the higher octaves of the etheric plane.

Just outside the etheric body is what I call the *astral shell*. The astral shell is a sheath that serves as the outer skin of the etheric, mental, emotional, and physical bodies. It's actually a duplicate of your physical self as it is now, rather than as it might be at the perfected level of your Higher Self.

A Delicate Time for the Soul

So now let's consider what happens to your four lower bodies at the change called death. The physical body ceases to function. The astral shell begins a decay process, and the human soul must determine where to go. During the delicate time between physical death and when a soul may enter devachan if she has merit, the soul is magnetized either up or down. The body that you find yourself in after death may be the etheric body or the emotional body. The mental body will be an adjunct to whichever body you gravitate to. You are always taking your mind with whatever body you occupy, including the physical.

Electronic belt, repository of the records of negative karma

The lower half of the three invisible bodies (etheric, mental, and emotional, or astral) is the seat of animal desire or passion. If you visualize a line drawn horizontally across the middle of the physical body, you would find that the lower nature is in the lower half of the etheric body, the lower half of the desire body, the lower half of the mental body, and the lower half of the physical body.

The negatives of your lower nature tend to gravitate toward the lower half and collect there, becoming a heavy weight. This is the repository of the records of negative karma, which I call the *electronic belt* (see page 59). It is the place of subconscious and unconscious records. The positive records rise to increase the level of your God Presence above.

If the soul has lived a generally good life, she* will not be attracted to her lower nature in the electronic belt and may enter devachan. If she does enter devachan, her negative karma is then sealed and awaits her return for her next incarnation. But if the soul has completely neglected spirituality, she is in danger of being attracted to the negative karma in her lower nature. If she remains with this lower nature, she is not sealed. This soul may be subject to malevolent spirits and may be drawn down into the dark vortices of the astral plane and lost for a time.

Freeing the Soul from the Body

After death, the astral shell (the outer skin of the etheric, mental, emotional, and physical bodies) is no longer needed and may be consumed along with the physical body through cremation, which I recommend, and the prayers and calls of loved ones. The combination of spiritual fire called forth by prayer along with the physical fire from the process of cremation will

---

*The soul of both man and woman is feminine in relation to the masculine, or spirit, portion of our being. The soul is therefore sometimes referred to in this book as "she" or "her."

free the soul to separate from the astral shell.

With the traditional ritual of the burial of the body, the light remains in the body, and the soul tends to be attached to the physical body. Then you have loved ones remaining who hold on to the person and continue to look for them, wanting to see and hear them. Friends and family sometimes go to séances to receive messages, and they exert such a strong pull upon the soul that she can scarcely get free to move on.

I think that cremation by fire is the way that the soul most easily gets free from the emotional attachments to the body. It also helps the family and loved ones, who remain to work through their attachment to the departed person and to contemplate the soul moving into the light of heavenly octaves.

....

A March 2019 *Wall Street Journal* article titled "The Free-Form Funeral" noted that cremations now outnumber burials in the U.S. The National Funeral Directors Association projected that by 2025 cremations would reach 64 percent. Although *WSJ* related this to a Pew Research Center survey showing a simultaneous steep rise in the percentage of Americans who say they are religiously "unaffiliated," one non-practicing Catholic said that her restaurant memorial gathering with dinner and her father's favorite beer left her feeling "something was missing" and that she does "find peace in some rituals and funerals." Another person, struggling with her husband's family tradition of cremation and scattering the ashes over a pasture on their farm, months later added a family gathering to plant a tree there to visit and tend. It's clear that, whether affiliated with a church or not, people have strong spiritual feelings. One funeral director said he observed a shift toward cremation in the 1990s and chalked it up to American "individualism."[4]

....

The physical body needs to pass through the flame so that its particles can be repolarized, recharged, and used again in creation. This, of course, is why we pass through the change called death. The bodies we wear have become used and tired, and it is time for all of their atoms to recycle.

In the process of cremation, the fire not only dissolves the physical form but may also erase many harmful records from the four lower bodies. The physical fire can affect these finer bodies and eliminate some of the very burdensome records and traumas that have occurred.

The Lowest Plane for Contact with God

We are living in physical bodies that correspond with a certain wavelength or vibration. The reason we're all here together on this ship of fools,[5] as they say, is that we all have a similar karma. We have similar things to do. We all have need of these bodies that we wear so that we can fulfill our divine plan, which is a requirement before we can reunite with God in the ritual of the ascension.

An evolution functioning at any lower level than the one we are in today could no longer actually make personal contact with the living God. If you look at the lowest of the low of evolutions on the physical earth today, you realize that if they were in any lower vibration—meaning more dense, less humanlike and more animallike—they actually would not have the means within themselves to contact God.

Therefore we have a tremendous opportunity. Although we are in the lowly estate of the flesh, in bodies that wear out in time and face many challenges, the one great gift we have is a living contact with God that we can establish and maintain through our Higher Self.

Is it possible for us to reach the level of other evolutions, such as that on Venus, who are more advanced than we are—those who have overcome war, who have greater spiritual light in their spiritual centers, a closer bonding to their Higher Self? I am not talking about those who are scientifically advanced. I am not talking about those who, just because they can, move around in spacecraft and do all kinds of scientific feats. I am talking about *spiritual* advancement, advancement in individual self-mastery where, most of all, we are Christlike beings. This is what will raise us to the level of life on Venus. We can live life on Earth at that level if we make right choices. Does that sound impossible to you?

The Physical Is the Crossroads

The physical plane is a very narrow band of experience. When you think about what we are able to see and experience, you have to realize that it is very narrow. Our physical eyes only see in the spectrum of visible light. There is much that is above and below what we are able to see in the physical plane. From the level of the conscious mind, rising upward in vibration, is the etheric plane. At a lower frequency than the physical is the astral plane. And the integration of the etheric and the astral is through the physical plane.

What you need to know about living in the physical plane is that these three planes—the etheric, astral, and physical—are overlapping. If you had the ability right now as a spiritual adept, you could be standing in this room in the same body you are now wearing but have full conscious awareness of higher octaves. You could live and move and have your being in realms of light. On the other hand, if you were dedicated to darkness, you could be integrated with the astral plane while in a physical body.

If you are perceptive and sensitive to people's auras and vibrations as you move through the cities of earth, through the subways, through various areas, you have a sense of those people who are carrying light and who are integrated with higher levels of being. You also have a sense of those whose vibrations are low. Think about this and take a look at your world. Remember that the astral plane has become an accumulation of the negative thoughts and emotions of all humanity for so long that it is like an ocean filled with pollution. This is why it's not where you want to dwell.

Many people in the world today are already integrated with the lower astral planes. They live on the astral plane here in the physical world. Everything they do in their waking state and in their sleeping state is carried on in these lower vibrations. Sometimes this comes about through drug, alcohol, or all kinds of other seemingly innocent addictions in which a person becomes unable to hold spiritual light or a spiritual flame. This is a danger for our youth and our nation and for the peoples of the whole world— the various addictions that people have as well as the various chemicals that they take in. Then there is the low vibration of just plain dedication to malice and to making life hard for others.

If you feel that you are sinking into astral levels, it may be that you have mixed with people who are inclined toward certain interests and pursuits of various kinds. You could probably make a list of the types of things that lower your vibration. If you tie yourself to people who have integrated with the astral plane, they will pull you down unless you are extremely strong and can pull them up. But many people who are in the astral plane are not interested in being pulled up. They just want to pull you down because they like to keep company with you. After all, you may have light that they can use since they are disconnected from their Higher Self and have no source to provide light.

Take a good look at those people to whom you are tied in your life, whether they are friends, work associates, or casual social contacts. Be sure that any who are largely centered in the astral plane are not sapping your light because you are open to them. Many people who dwell in astral levels have no desire to be anywhere else because they are very comfortable there.

So the physical plane is the crossroads. And as long as you are in physical incarnation on earth, you can decide to do an about-face, and you can divest yourself of these lower astral vibrations. Then you can enter into the vibrations of your Higher Self.

Enter the Golden Ages

Buddhists want to be reborn in Tushita heaven to personally receive teachings from their guru. But it is possible to experience the highest octaves of light while we are still in this physical body. We can attain samadhi or nirvana, and we can enter the golden ages that are now in progress in etheric octaves. If we choose to qualify ourselves, we can dwell *in consciousness* in Tushita heaven, where Maitreya is instructing his bodhisattvas. But you will not achieve this unless you have been accepted and initiated by Maitreya.

If you have studied the elements of historical Buddhism, remember that Maitreya is not so relevant to us as a past bodhisattva or a future Buddha. But he is gloriously relevant to us as a very present spiritual master having full Buddhahood. In truth, Maitreya has been a Buddha since the hour of his ascension in 531 B.C.

Therefore, in the splendor of the Buddhas, we can claim the truth of the Buddha Maitreya's presence with us and affirm: "My teacher, my friend, Maitreya, lives within me, and I AM his representative where I AM." When you say, "I AM," you are referring to God within you, the divine spark that God has placed within your heart. Then you can be Maitreya in action in your daily life and in your service to life.

Or you could just as easily say, "My teacher, my friend, Jesus, lives within me and I AM his representative where I AM." When you question, "What would Jesus do?" and you strive to live by his standard, it's the same principle of the master-disciple relationship.

Jesus the Christ *Maitreya*

Maitreya's devotees know that the personal encounter with him will accelerate them on the bodhisattva path. Though desiring to be reborn in Tushita heaven is a legitimate aim, it can also be somewhat of a procrastination. This happens in Christianity and in other spiritual traditions as well. Unless you know better, this dream of a future paradise with Jesus, with Maitreya, with saints and spiritual teachers, may lull you into sleepfulness instead of saying: "I can know my teacher, my spiritual master, right here and now, right where I am today. Furthermore, my soul can rise to the etheric plane and consciousness of my own Higher Self, where I may encounter my teacher face-to-face!"

To fail to affirm this possibility here and now is to tie in to the human tendency to postpone, for whatever reason, the great encounter with a spiritual teacher. And this tendency follows us, or we follow it, through the world's religions. We tend to postpone this encounter not because of religious doctrine but because of our own personal psychology.

You Can Begin Right Now

You can make up your own affirmations spontaneously in order to raise your consciousness to etheric levels right now. Say them with all the fire of your heart. Begin your affirmations of light with the name "I AM," which means "God in me is."

For example, you can get up in the morning and say, "I AM a son of God! I AM full of joy! I AM love in action today! I AM going forth to conquer my day! I AM grateful for the abundance in my life!" You can just keep on affirming that God within you (remembering that God is energy) is going to manifest in everything that you desire to accomplish, including the bringing of a bit more of heaven to earth.

You can affirm your life right now as a victorious manifestation of God. See yourself seated in a sphere of white light and try giving this in full voice:[6]

I AM Light

I AM light, glowing light,
Radiating light, intensified light.
God consumes my darkness,
Transmuting it into light.
This day I AM a focus of the Central Sun.
Flowing through me is a crystal river,
A living fountain of light
That can never be qualified
By human thought and feeling.
I AM an outpost of the Divine.
Such darkness as has used me is swallowed up
By the mighty river of light which I AM.
I AM, I AM, I AM light;
I live, I live, I live in light.

I AM light's fullest dimension;
I AM light's purest intention.
I AM light, light, light
Flooding the world everywhere I move,
Blessing, strengthening, and conveying
The purpose of the kingdom of heaven.

This set of affirmations can be the alchemy for personal change such as you would never have believed or dreamed could happen in your world. God within you is the affirmation, the speaking of the words, and also the fulfillment of the Word of God. Feel God giving these affirmations through you. It is as if he drops a portion of himself as a pebble in the pond of your being, and the ripples go forth from you in concentric rings. When they reach the shore, they return to the center. And their returning to the center is like the echo of God. As his voice has gone forth from you, so it will return to you with that fulfillment and that supreme joy of living on earth here and now in the God flame within your heart.

Sometimes people feel that a mystical understanding of Jesus Christ or of Gautama Buddha is beyond their ability. Perhaps they feel that they are not educated enough to understand. If you think that you are one of these people, or if you feel you do not have the capacity to understand, perish the thought. God lives in you and his mind is in you. His mind will open in answer to your prayer and by your flowing with the stream of his consciousness by your giving of the Word.

Can you imagine that God would create us without this innate formula of understanding and of knowing the path back Home? I can only remind you of the great storehouse of truth that God has already placed within you.

Spiritual Study While You Sleep

You can live at an etheric level while you are still in a physical body on earth, but you can also aim for even higher levels after you make the transition called death. An experience in devachan may be necessary for some people's soul evolution. But it is not the shortest distance between two points for those who are seriously on the path of their soul's reunion with God. The best place to go is to the higher etheric levels of the heaven-world, where you can be with the ascended masters, learning from them in their retreats from the moment of your transition.

You can also study in spiritual retreats through soul travel when you lay your body down to rest at night. I have written a book called *Lords of the Seven Rays*. It describes these spiritual masters and their retreats and gives you an idea of what each of them teaches. (See page 210, Appendix A, for a chart that gives more about these seven masters.) You can ask Archangel Michael to take you to these retreats as you fall asleep at night.

The etheric body is the vehicle in which your soul travels to get to that higher level during sleep—if you have the momentum of light so that you can get there. Not everyone reaches that level. If you are involved in lower states of consciousness such as we discussed earlier, you will not gravitate to the etheric plane while you sleep. Instead you will gravitate to the astral plane. Having a bad dream at night, although it may be conditioned by your own subconscious and an acid stomach, still may denote some equivalency in your state of consciousness to the astral plane. In that case, you would be traveling in your emotional body rather than in your etheric body. That's the difference between those two experiences. And similarly, those who have near-death experiences may go out in the etheric body or they may go out in the emotional body.

In order to be sure you get to these retreats, you need to raise your consciousness, and you need protection. You can ask Archangel Michael to seal and protect you while your body sleeps and for his blue-lightning angels to escort you to and from these spiritual retreats. You also may want to have a picture of the spiritual master of your choice or of the geographic location over which the master has an etheric retreat to meditate upon before retiring.

It is a worthy goal to be tutored under the ascended masters, who have fulfilled their reason for being and reunited with God. But the masters require us to create a bridge from our world to theirs. We build that bridge through service to their cause, which is the cause of peace and the liberation of all souls. They require that we give service to life and that we give devotions through prayer, meditation, and mantras. By focusing our energy in devotions, we build a cord of light whereby we can sustain a strong tie to the etheric octave and therefore keep open the doors of the student-teacher relationship. As the saying goes, "When the student is ready, the teacher will appear."

These devotions will also keep you tied to your Higher Self and to your God Presence, neither of which will ever descend into this physical plane. We have to rise in consciousness to that etheric level to be one with them. And if we want to commune with the ascended masters, we must make our abode in that etheric octave even as we walk in the physical plane on earth.

You may visit the retreats for some time before having a waking memory of an experience there. If this is so, do not be concerned. You may return with a prompting, a feeling, or an inner direction about decisions to be made in your life without realizing where the prompting came from. Retreat experiences and service with the masters on the etheric plane may also come to your outer awareness as the recall of a particularly vivid dream.

Cities of the Etheric Realm

With a momentum of going to the spiritual retreats while you sleep at night, your soul may gravitate more easily to the great cities of light in the etheric plane located at various points on the planet when you pass on. In these etheric cities we find individuals who are preparing to incarnate, who must wait for the opportune moment when the gates of birth are opened to them and they can once again come forth to work out their destiny in the world of form. These waiting souls live and work and serve in situations not unlike those they have left on earth, with the exception that the etheric cities hold the pattern for what the physical is intended to be in a golden age. There are universities of the Spirit, great temples of light, and homes similar to those we know on earth. There are temples of worship, of healing, of invocation and purification, of ideal forms of government, of education, of art, and of music.

Those who spend their time between incarnations in these cities have a great worth to contribute in their succeeding lives. Those who carry the flame of idealism in their next incarnation do so out of the remembrance of the joy and happiness they experienced in living, perhaps for centuries, in these etheric homes of light. They come "trailing clouds of glory" in the great hope that somewhere on this green earth they can re-create the beauty and peace they have known in the higher octaves.

The etheric cities show us what the previous golden ages on earth looked like and how the world can be again in a future golden age. A high percentage of the souls who visit the etheric cities try to bring forth some aspects of these cities when they return to earth. Great training and preparation is given to souls who live in these cities and who spend time studying in the retreats of the masters.

We need to establish institutions and facilities of higher education on earth that will enable incoming souls to bring forth that which they have learned in the higher octaves. This is what it will take to bring us closer to having a golden age.

CHAPTER 4

The Dangers of Discarnates

He's stuck. That's what it is. He's in between worlds. . . .
It happens sometimes that the spirit gets yanked out so
fast that the essence still feels it has work to do here.

ODA MAE BROWN IN THE MOVIE *GHOST*

Our exploration of the afterlife would not be complete without considering the important topic of discarnates. In chapter 2, I said that discarnates are those who have passed on, no longer have a physical body, and remain in the lower levels near the physical earth. Dr. Moody refers to discarnates as "bewildered spirits," and they are also sometimes called "disembodied spirits" or "discarnate entities." They are made up of the personality consciousness of those who have passed through the change called death as that consciousness expresses itself through the astral, mental, or etheric bodies.

The movie *Ghost*[1] is a great taking-off point for a closer look at this subject, as it depicts fairly accurately what happens on this level of existence. Before we delve into this movie and what it can show us about the world of discarnates, let's briefly review some of the key points we've covered so far to set the stage.

When a person passes on and has not yet earned the right to remain in the heaven-world, which is the goal of life, they must prepare to return to embodiment again or, in other words, prepare to reincarnate. The more advanced souls are taken to the etheric retreats between incarnations to further develop their existing talents and to acquire new talents for future service. Not all who pass on through the change called death reach these etheric schoolrooms. Many get stuck in the astral plane, where their energies remain entangled with embodied and disembodied souls who carry the lowest common denominator of human vibration.

Souls who lack the necessary spiritual momentum to rise to the etheric octave after death may hover around their old familiar places, in most cases unable to communicate with those they have left behind. This is extremely frustrating to discarnates, especially when they are unaware that they are dead. They are fully conscious of the physical world around them and can move among the living, but they are unnoticed and almost totally ignored—except when they can indirectly influence incarnate individuals, those who still have physical bodies, by tying in to their feeling worlds.

Some souls have such a heavy karma that they reincarnate directly from the astral plane. They never go anywhere. They do not advance spiritually. They come back basically as they were, with the same habits, the same desires, the same momentums.

You can see why I have said how important it is to pray for those who pass on in our families so that they will be taken to the highest possible place. The hope of progress is in the spiritual retreats. And thus I have a profound compassion and desire to see this teaching spread far and wide And thus I have a profound compassion and desire to see this teaching spread far and wide so that people are aware of these retreats and know how to prepare to get there when it is time for their passing.

One thing is sure in life, beyond paying taxes: the transition called death awaits us all. This transition can be a terrifying prospect, or it can be made in the highest wisdom, love and light.

Discarnates in the Movie *Ghost*

The movie *Ghost* gives a very realistic picture of the death process and the discarnate that separates from the body at that point of transition. It's the story of a New York banker, Sam Wheat, who is killed by a mugger. After Sam realizes that he is dead and discovers that he has been murdered, he follows the mugger who killed him. Sam eventually learns that Carl, his business associate, hired the mugger and is now going after Sam's girlfriend, Molly Jenson. Sam, now a discarnate, works at protecting Molly and solving the crime. At the end of the movie, after Sam has succeeded in keeping Molly safe and bringing Carl and the mugger to justice, his spirit gradually dissolves into light, presumably going to heaven.

This movie makes a number of statements about life after death that I would like to examine for you in greater detail. First of all, the movie shows that people can be bewildered and disoriented after death. The newly dead often stay in the astral plane in or near their former home, and they have difficulty moving around. All of this is absolutely true. You might be shocked to hear this, but there are billions of discarnates on the earth today who are not in the afterlife level where they belong. This is especially true in large cities where there are so many people dying on a daily basis.

Sam's death takes place when he is attacked as he and Molly walk home at night after seeing a play. As Sam fights with the attacker and tries to protect Molly, he is shot. Then we see him chasing the fleeing attacker. When he turns around to see what has happened to Molly, he realizes that his body is on the ground in Molly's arms and that she is screaming for help. Molly is shouting his name and asking him to respond, but he cannot. Sam watches the ambulance come and take his body to the hospital as he slowly realizes that he is dead.

You might think that death is an instantaneous awareness. But I've seen people at the scene of accidents, sudden accidents that come to people of all ages, where they have tried to get back into their physical body or have remained at the scene of the accident trying to figure out what happened to them or trying to make the car start. They will stay at the scene, totally in a state of mind of bewilderment, not able to navigate. They do not realize that they have been separated from their body. Sometimes it takes days, weeks, or extended periods of time for people to actually recognize that they have made their transition.

Sam follows his body to the hospital and sits dumbfounded in a waiting-room chair as Molly is told that there is no hope. Another discarnate sits next to Sam and explains what is happening with other people dying. This is typical of what you might see if you were clairvoyant. For the first few days after he dies, Sam stays in his apartment. He cannot go through doors unless people have opened them.

Sam attends his own funeral. People often really do attend their own funerals. It's almost a necessary process, just as it's necessary for loved ones who remain to recognize that there is a finality here, and a parting. While Sam is at his own funeral, he is shocked to see a woman across the graveyard waving to him. But then she walks through a tombstone, and Sam realizes that she too is in the realm of the dead.

At his apartment Sam tries to communicate with Molly, but to no avail. He tries to touch her, but she walks right through him. After that, he just sits in the windowsill or in the corner, like a forlorn child, unable to make himself heard. This is quite a bit like how it feels to suddenly find oneself without a body on the astral plane and to not understand what is going on.

Some Truth and Some Error

The movie makes the point that after people die, if they have been generally good, they are taken to a place with light and good spirits, but if they have been evil, they are taken by dark spirits. If they think that they have something left to do or if they are attached to their loved ones and their surroundings, some people can choose to remain as discarnates on earth. This idea is basically true, but there is some error to it also. I'll give you examples of what the movie shows, and then I'll give you an interpretation of it.

When Sam dies, he looks up at the sky and sees twinkling lights that remain suspended above him for a moment. He seems to know that this is where he should be going, and he hears the call to come to the heaven-world. But he is not ready to leave Molly, who is pleading with him not to leave her. He makes a freewill decision to stay, and then the lights disappear. This really does happen. The angels do bow to free will and leave you where you want to be. I've seen this happen time and time again, where angels come to take souls to higher octaves but some individuals refuse to go.

After Sam succeeds in protecting Molly, he is ready to be taken to where he is supposed to go, and the twinkling lights appear again for a few moments. While these lights are present, Molly begins to hear him for the first time and his form gradually appears to her, surrounded by light. Oda Mae then tells Sam, "They're waiting for you." Sam hesitates, looks at Molly and tells her, "It's amazing, Molly. The love inside—you take it with you." Then he turns away to dissolve into a realm of light.

At one point in *Ghost,* Sam observes a man dying in the emergency room as twinkling lights descend to take the man's spirit up right away. Other discarnates, such as a man he meets on the subway, stay near familiar places indefinitely. But not everyone can choose to stay. When Carl and the mugger he hired die, instead of twinkling lights coming to get them, howling and shrieking demons emerge from the ground and drag them away, presumably to the realms of hell.

This picture is not entirely accurate. My observation is that the legions of Archangel Michael come and forcibly bind souls who have committed great evil so that they cannot work further harm. The angels then consign these souls to one of the thirty-three levels of the astral plane.

But it is possible that there are evil spirits around that desire to take those whom they think belong to them into the astral plane. In some cases where individuals have devoted their lives to evil, they can continue to roam and work harm, doing very deadly deeds after they pass on. These discarnates are deadly because they are operating from the level of adeptship in the black arts. They can cause fires. They can cause deaths to happen. But in answer to our prayers and calls, these dangerous discarnates can be bound and taken away so that they cannot cause harm. So there are many, many possible scenarios, as you can imagine, even as there are many different souls.

Observable Phenomena

Some discarnates in the movie *Ghost* are capable of moving physical objects. While Sam is following his murderer, he encounters a tall, frightening discarnate on a subway car. The discarnate picks him up and throws him out of the car, telling him not to come into his territory again. To frighten Sam, the spirit smashes one of the subway windows. He has mastered the technique of doing things with physical objects.

Later in the movie, Sam seeks out the subway discarnate and demands that he teach him how to move objects around. As Sam is trying to move physical things, this discarnate reminds him, "You ain't got a body now, son. It's all up here now." The discarnate points to his head. "If you want to move something, you've gotta move it with your mind. You've gotta focus. You've gotta take all your emotions, all your anger, all your love, all your hate, and push it down here into the pit of your stomach and let it explode like a reactor." The discarnate demonstrates by forcefully "kicking" a can across the ground.

Sam makes this tremendous effort to focus all of the energy that he has, and he eventually succeeds in learning how to move objects. He spends time practicing kicking cans and moving other objects. In the course of the movie, he turns a stove off, closes doors, and types on a computer. To convince Molly that he is real, he even pushes a penny up a door and carries it on his finger to her. Molly sees the penny float through the air to her hand. Later, in order to protect Molly, Sam is even able to punch and knock down the man who had killed him.

There are many examples of psychic phenomena that have been traced to discarnates called *poltergeists,* which means "noisy ghosts." Examples of such phenomena are chairs rocking, voices speaking, and things happening in houses. This is the nature of discarnates that hang around. They may or may not be able to move physical objects. But they are certainly not invulnerable, and they need to be taken by angels to their rightful place. That's why our prayers and calls to clear the earth of these discarnates are so important.

My advice to you is not to be fascinated with death or with any of the things I've described. Just learn how to do the spiritual work so that none of these things need to be a part of you, your household, your office, or wherever you're staying or spending time.

Craving Former Pleasures

The movie *Ghost* also shows a discarnate craving the pleasures he had while he was in human form. When Sam is getting his training from the subway discarnate, the discarnate kicks out the window of a cigarette vending machine. Kneeling and looking at all the packs of cigarettes on the ground he says, "I'd give *anything* for a drag, just one drag." But of course he cannot smoke, because he has no physical body.

This is absolutely true and a very important story to be told. Discarnate entities crave the sensual pleasures to which they were addicted before losing their physical bodies, so they attach themselves to people on earth in order to experience life vicariously. The law of attraction (like attracts like) governs the movement of these discarnate entities, who gravitate toward energy pools of a similar vibration.

Just think about it. Entities of self-pity gravitate toward people who have self-pity, and so on, including any human vibration you want to name. If you are in a certain negative vibration, or state of consciousness, you will attract discarnate entities that are in this same state. But if you have light's protection around you, you will not attract discarnates. You will attract angels and higher beings instead. The law of attraction is a serious matter, and that's why you need to be careful about your state of consciousness. Discarnate entities move compulsively, merging with other misqualified bodies of energy that roam the astral world until they find shelter in the auras of like-minded incarnate individuals.

People who do not have any kind of spiritual practice at all usually have some kind of entity around them that is so similar to

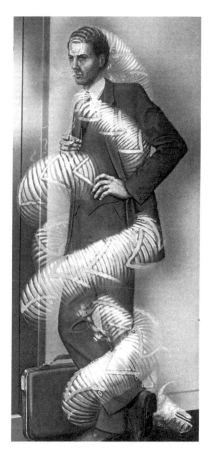

Smoker with astral tobacco entity

themselves that they cannot even tell it's there. They assume that the discarnate's thoughts and feelings are their own. This may be in part because their thoughts and feelings reflect those of a discarnate entity that is very much like them. Again, like attracts like.

Few among us are free from the influence of discarnate entities. Discarnate entities that perhaps have been around us for more than one lifetime feel threatened if we want to change a habit or addiction. So entities who are used to sapping our light are not going to take kindly to our deciding to be entity-free for the rest of our life.

A New Look at Habits and Addictions

Consider people addicted to alcohol, tobacco, drugs, or excessive sugar, for example. Astral entities are attracted to those on the physical plane who have habit patterns similar to their own. Bars and hangouts of drug users are literally packed with discarnates who attach themselves to those who are taking in these substances. Sometimes as many as fifty to a hundred entities attach themselves like leeches to one individual who is smoking or taking drugs. And by attaching themselves to an incarnate person, these discarnate entities can experience smoking that cigarette, taking that drink of alcohol, taking that cocaine or whatever.

In order to experience these highs, discarnates hook into people in physical incarnation at the base of the skull and upper vertebrae of the body. By so doing, they lock into the incarnate person's central nervous system and vicariously enjoy the pleasures to which they are accustomed. This transfer takes place as the result of the merging of the astral bodies of the discarnates with the astral and physical bodies of the incarnate individual through the sympathetic nervous system.

The desire of an individual for alcohol or other harmful substances can be multiplied as much as a thousand times by the desires of entities. I have now just given you a new definition of addiction. People find it impossible to stop smoking, to stop drinking, to stop the sugar habit, to stop the drug habit, to stop being completely careless in their sexual habits—even if they know that they may die—all because these discarnate entities tie in to them. Discarnates urge people and goad them to engage in the discarnate's addictions and habits.

The actions of such entities greatly exacerbate the problems of addiction. Not only must the individual fight his own cravings, but he must fight the cravings of a whole host of discarnates who latch on to him. For instance, someone can be enslaved not only by heroin or opioids themselves but also by powerful astral forces. There are demons and fallen angels who go about luring people of all ages to take heroin and become addicted to it. This is of course true of every other type of drug on the planet.

This is why, when you are praying for yourself or for someone else, you need to call to Archangel Michael to bind all demons and discarnates who have become possessing entities. Entities can possess a person and take over his life. People may feel that they just cannot exist unless they can go out and smoke every two hours or indulge in whatever their addiction is. They want to stop, but they can't stop.

If you call with determination for the help and intercession of Archangel Michael, you will be surprised by what miracles can happen—how a person can be immediately freed from these harmful substances because the legions of light remove those entities. When you are free of entities, your own desire is all you have to deal with. And you can work on that more easily.

Communicating with the Other Side

Moving on with our analysis of *Ghost,* we see that Sam has to solve the murder by himself. Molly knows the murderer but does not suspect him, since she and Sam were both friends of his. Sam is concerned that his murderer will now murder Molly because she is getting too close to finding out about Carl's money laundering for a drug trafficker.

Sam goes to a spiritualist medium in order to communicate with Molly. The medium, Oda Mae Brown, is played by Whoopi Goldberg, and it's a very humorous scene. Sam wants Oda Mae to help him warn Molly. At first she refuses, but he keeps her awake all night with raucous singing, and she finally agrees to help him.

Throughout the movie, Sam goes to see Oda Mae. At one point he interrupts a séance attended by people and about ten discarnates. Oda Mae had been a fake for years. But when Sam came along, she started to really hear discarnates, and so now her place is packed with them. In the midst of this confusion, an impatient spirit jumps into Oda Mae's body and begins speaking through her. Suddenly her voice is the voice of a man.

So the movie shows discarnates talking to and sometimes using the body of a spiritualist medium, or psychic. It's absolutely true that mediums or psychics can give messages from discarnate entities to whoever wants to hear them. I recommend that you do not engage in this activity because it ties you into the astral world. It also ties you into a sympathetic and symbiotic relationship to someone who has passed on and who needs to be moving on with their soul evolution.

The veil between this world and the next is thin, almost like a gossamer veil, and it is possible to commune with loved ones. But when people pass on, there is a finality for that life. We need to surrender our loved ones and continue living, as hard as it may seem to do so. The departed have other schoolrooms in the heaven-world where they will be learning and growing. They have a new life and need to move on.

Draining of the Life Force

When Oda Mae says to the discarnate, "Get out of me!" he leaves her body and lies limply on the floor and has no energy to move. His fellow discarnate ridicules him for not knowing that entering a physical body drains a discarnate of energy.

This is where the fallacy lies, and this is where the danger is. What the movie does not reveal is that discarnates drain energy *from* the medium. And that is why you do not want to be going to séances if you have spiritual goals. The vital energies that are taken by the spirits from those who participate—whether as a medium or an observer—are never replaced. Those energies are immediately used to produce psychic phenomena and to sustain the existence of these discarnate entities.

As far as I am concerned, there is no difference between a spiritualist, or psychic medium, and a channeler. I do not judge them. I personally know many people engaged in this service who are dedicated to it. I love them and I bless them. But I want you to know that this practice is dangerous.

If people consciously practice communion with the dead or hold consort with the spirits of the departed over a considerable period of time, their vital spiritual energies will gradually be drained. A deterioration of the physical body and the brain will take place. Each of us has a certain allotment of the life force that is apportioned to us at the beginning of our incarnation. Prolonged involvement in trance work, psychic phenomena, and spiritualistic activities can result in a critical drain upon that allotment.

We are intended to use the energy of light that surrounds the body (in our aura) and that is in the body to weave a kind of garment that I call the deathless solar body. This body is required in order for us to be able to enter the higher etheric levels at the time of our transition.

Real-Life Examples

I used to know a very sweet lady who was a spiritualist medium. She had dedicated her life to receiving messages and had her circle of people who came to her home, which was so packed with discarnate entities that it was unbelievable.

Every so many months she would call me, tell me that she was very sick, and ask if I would please pray for her. Well, I knew exactly what was happening. So I would call to Archangel Michael to clear the entities out of her house and off her body. Then she'd call me and say she was feeling fine. This would last for another three months or four months of séances, but then she would call me again.

She was bound and determined to help all these discarnates receive comfort, receive teaching, receive healing, bless her heart. She believed to her dying day that she was rendering a tremendous service to all of them, but what she was really doing was keeping the discarnates earthbound and tied to her. When you come right down to it, this was almost a point of ego.

I know of another case of two very devout souls, a husband and wife, who were the sweetest people that you would ever want to meet. Yet they lacked a certain energy, a certain layer of light that is natural to the aura of those on the spiritual path. This was because they had been psychics and were involved in spiritualism in past lives.

Unfortunately, I could see that it would take this couple four or five lifetimes to regain the light squandered in that activity. I trust, however, that they have made great progress on the spiritual path. But it is an amazing example. You could see that something was missing, even though they were lovely people.

What about Channeling?

There is extreme danger in channeling astral entities purporting to be masters and spiritual guides. Discarnates who profess to be masters of the psychic realm are the most dangerous of all. They not only drain the vital energies of their auditors, but they lead people astray by releasing confusing information and half-truths. They may present even as much as 70 or 80 percent truth. Because that much of what they say is so plainly true, many people tend to accept the percentage of error that is expressed.

An entity that speaks to and through a channeler is likely to be a deceased person's astral shell, which can exist separately from the soul and even make negative karma for which the soul is accountable. It can often make accurate psychic predictions, but it is not omniscient. For a short time after the transition called death, the astral shell of a disembodied soul experiences a flash of expanded awareness, a sense of all-knowingness that can be prophetic. The soul, however, does not receive this as a permanent gift until she ascends to God after her final incarnation.

Contrary to what you might believe, discarnate entities cannot (as a rule) assist us in finding our soul freedom. They themselves are not free, and therefore they cannot give true soul freedom to others. If they had spiritual attainment, they would not be hovering near the earth.

Messengers of the ascended masters do not give what are known as life readings except in certain circumstances. There is a big difference between channeling disembodied spirits and receiving teachings through the Holy Spirit from ascended masters, who are God-free beings. I do not consider that I have psychic powers or even clairvoyance. What I have is the mantle of messenger. That mantle is a grid of light that is around me to protect me from receiving teachings from any but the ascended hosts of light.

Partial life readings taken from the astral level by psychics (for want of any other word) are dangerous for a number of reasons. I don't use the word *psychic* as a pejorative. I'm using it here for someone who has awakened and quickened soul senses. If the soul is awakened, it is essential that she rise and become one with her Higher Self in order to avoid such entanglements with astral levels.

I have seen many people who have had life readings and who came to me with a great burden after being told that they were a certain person or did something in a past life. In order to assist them on their spiritual path, I have asked the ascended masters and discovered many times that they were not that person at all. But ever since they had visited someone who did a past-life regression, they had believed it and carried a burden that wasn't even theirs to carry or they had illusions of grandeur that were totally ridiculous.

The worst part of regressions is when it actually is one of their past lives and the person is totally unequipped to deal with the horrendous experience that occurred. If the person is not ready for this step on their spiritual path, then this information can be very unhealthy for them. It's like forcing a flower to bloom.

Until God reveals a past life to you because the time has come for you to deal with that karma, leave it alone. Don't be curious about it. You are who you are today, the sum total of all your past lives.

Spiritual Pride

Alcoholics, drug addicts, chain-smokers, et cetera, are not the only victims of the wiles of discarnate entities. Entities have a trap for every type of human consciousness, even for those who consider themselves the elect of God. The vibrations of spiritual pride can also attract to the aspirant the most deadly type of entities who seek nothing short of the destruction of the soul.

Spiritual pride is that which is embodied by a "higher" type of discarnate entity on the left-handed path, such as black magicians who are very subtle and very cunning in the thoughts that they project into your mind and that you agree with because you are not yet purified from intellectual, human, spiritual, or whatever type of pride. Because you think that these entities have a lot of knowledge about spiritual matters, you can, through the magnetic quality of wishful thinking concerning your own spiritual mastery, put yourself into a serious karma-making situation with other people who count upon you for guidance, even though you mean well.

So some people may not be addicted to the lower order of things that we're speaking of (drugs, tobacco, sugar, etc.), yet they may be addicted to *themselves*. Therefore they are susceptible to entities that have the same type of thought and feeling processes that they have. Spiritual pride is a blinding force, and often those enmeshed in it cannot see it or its dangers.

You have the resources. You don't have to be taken in by the flattery of getting special messages from a discarnate claiming to be a master. You can call to Archangel Michael and his blue-lightning angels to remove imposters, with a call something like this:

In the name of Almighty God, I demand the binding of all discarnates and fallen angels who would dare to come near and impose themselves upon me. I call to Archangel Michael to seize all entities that are not of the light and to remove them from my aura, my consciousness, my home, and my workplace. I refuse to accept the presence of anything less than the living God!

Discarnates Need Your Energy

Discarnate entities are tormented by their unfulfilled desires and are disconnected from their Higher Self and from God. Sooner or later they discover the means of drawing strength from those who have not lost their tie to their Source.

As I've discussed above, conscious, willing cooperation of people on earth who involve themselves with psychic activity and channeling is one way that discarnates can get our energy. But there are other seemingly innocent or normal human activities that can allow entities to sap our energy. Whenever we are inharmonious or out of tune with our Higher Self in any way, we are vulnerable. Vibrations of irritation, grief, fear, anger, gossip, envy, depression, disdain, fatigue, and other negative thoughts and feelings—even dissonant rhythms, sounds, and words in music—puncture the natural protective envelope placed around our souls at birth in order to hold the spiritual energies that are released to us from God. Discord of any kind in our world automatically rends, or tears, our spiritual garment. Without the wholeness of this spiritual protection, our energies become vulnerable to discarnate entities.

A common way that we may be out of tune with our Higher Self is through the foods that we eat even when we know they are harming us. Discarnates can get your energy if you overload your body with sugar, for instance. You become open, allowing entities to take your energy and light. This is why entities like to get people addicted to sugar.

The problem we have in the United States today is that cereals and processed foods of every kind have sugar or other harmful substances added to them. You need to read the labels on all of the food you buy and recognize that sugar comes in many guises and may be listed under a different name. Sugar in any form weakens you and makes you susceptible to the astral plane and to entities.

Entities are unable to attach themselves to those who are in tune with their Higher Self. If these entities can catch you off guard, though, they can derive more benefit from the relatively pure energies of those on the spiritual path than they can from those who move in and are saturated with the momentums of the astral plane. This is because the purer the energies, the more readily they are assimilated by the entity.

Signs of Vulnerability

Some time ago I knew a man who was having too many crazy accidents, stupid accidents that hurt him physically. He came to me and sincerely implored me to tell him why he was having these accidents.

In this particular case, his vulnerability came from holes in his spiritual garment, which, as I said earlier, is the natural protective envelope that surrounds our soul. The holes were the result of the misuse of God's energy and other things he had done in this life and previous lives. These holes needed to be mended. You can ask the angels to take the light you call forth in prayer and to weave a patch, so to speak, for any tears in the garment of your finer bodies. And of course, this man needed to conserve his life force and to avoid what caused the holes in the first place, as well as appeal to the healing angels to mend the tears.

I often see that drugs have caused holes in the spiritual garment of those just starting out on the spiritual path. And therefore much healing is required. Healing angels will assist you, your loved ones, and those for whom you pray. It is a necessary process.

Some people, because of what they've done in many lifetimes as well as in this one, have so many holes in their spiritual garment that they cannot retain the light from their spiritual devotions or practice for even twelve hours. It's like having a sieve for an aura. But this too can be healed. It can be mended. With God and with the light, all things are possible.

When the veil between the physical and the astral plane is punctured from any cause, it opens you to the astral plane in general and you can thereby become a magnet that attracts astral entities to you. Discarnate forces can then break through into the physical and cause sudden accidents and physical injury. These forces can also cause lesser intrusions that you may experience, such as having a bad day, getting a headache, or things just not going right. These are some of the ways that discarnates can affect you if you haven't invoked enough spiritual protection.

How to Heal

Anyone who has damaged their natural spiritual protection by any means can ask for God's forgiveness for having created a condition whereby they have become vulnerable to astral forces. For example, those who have been damaged by drug use can ask forgiveness for having interfered with the natural unfoldment of the divine plan within their lives. Then they can invoke

Archangel Michael and his legions of blue lightning to seal and protect them.

These people also need to pray for the reweaving of their spiritual garment, their aura. When matter and substance become distorted through disease and the wrong use of energy, those manifestations will continue as long as there is energy to sustain them.

If you call from the level of your Higher Self for your physical form to stop a wrong action, there can then be a dissolving of wrong thought patterns, and the original divine design that is within your Higher Self and God Presence can begin to be reestablished within you. An intense action for healing is compelled from octaves of light when you faithfully make the call for your own healing. All of us need healing at some level, whether we know it or not. So here is something you can use right now as a prayer, a meditation, or to give out loud.

Center in your heart and envision yourself within a white-fire core surrounded by a tangible, sapphire-blue sphere of light containing your original divine design and the will of God. See a globe of emerald-green healing light surrounding it all.

Your entire form is enfolded in God's healing Presence when your visualization is concentrated and charged with love as you give the following prayer. Remember that every time you use "I AM" you are declaring, "God in me is." Try saying this out loud:

Almighty God, in the name of my Higher Self, take command of my entire being. Create and sustain in me a perfect picture of the divine design. See that this action is established in my whole being and make me whole both now and forever. Work in me the fullness of a right mind in action to remove all distortions in my flesh form and my mental body, bringing about the wondrous purity of

*God as it descends. Kindle around me the aura of the
Infinite One until circling me is the angelic power of light.*

*I AM God's perfection manifest
In body, mind, and soul—
I AM God's direction flowing
To heal and keep me whole!*

*O atoms, cells, electrons
Within this form of mine,
Let heaven's own perfection
Make me now divine!
I charge and charge and charge myself
With radiant I AM light—
I feel the flow of purity
That now makes all things right!*

*In full faith I thankfully accept this manifest right here
and now with full power, eternally sustained, and all
powerfully active! Beloved I AM! Beloved I AM! Beloved
I AM!*

The healing process takes place through the restoration of
wholeness, first in your soul (both spiritually and emotionally),
then in your mind (mentally and visually), and finally in your
body, which will always reflect the state of your higher bodies.
What appears to be failure in achieving the results that we seek
is really that we have not held the vision of the perfect image
with determination long enough to see it come into being.
Whenever you pray for healing, know that the call compels the
answer. God will answer your prayer not necessarily as you have
envisioned the answer but at the time and in the way that your
soul truly needs.

CHAPTER 5

Taking Heaven by Force

Everything matters.
Everything we do matters.

NELSON IN THE MOVIE *FLATLINERS*

L et's turn now to another movie that can shed light on some of the key spiritual issues that underpin our understanding and experience of the afterlife—the movie *Flatliners*.[1] I have to confess that it was very difficult for me to watch this movie. I didn't enjoy the experience of going through dying and coming back four or five times. Yet I wanted to watch this movie so I could share my insights on it with you.

Flatliners teaches us about karma and resolution. Its message is summed up by Nelson, the main character, when he says, "Everything matters. Everything we do matters." Well, I say that if the churches won't teach people about karma, then let the movies teach it! This movie does have a number of shortcomings, but I will describe the characters and give you the story line along with my analysis.

A group of five medical students with high GPAs decide that they want to find out if there is really life after death. They are aware of near-death experiences, so they take turns using an injection and medical equipment to "kill" each other on different nights. After the person is dead for a certain number of minutes, the students use medical equipment to bring the person back to life.

One-by-one the students are hooked up to an EKG (electrocardiograph) and an EEG (electroencephalograph) so that they can determine when the heart stops beating and when the individual is brain-dead. The students lower the body temperature by the use of a refrigerated blanket in order to reduce the danger of permanent brain damage. They stop the heart by electric shocks that are administered by a defibrillator. When the person is dead, the EKG and EEG cease registering brain and heart waves—they flatline.

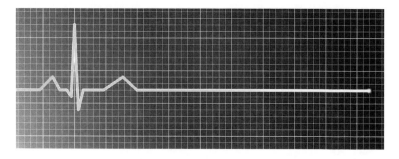

I asked a medical doctor to analyze their procedure. He said that it's certainly possible to kill someone in this way but that it's questionable that they all could have been successfully revived. "You never know whether someone's going to revive," he said. He also said that the speed of their recovery from death was unrealistic, as was the speed with which they raised and lowered their body temperatures. I won't take time to explain other plot weaknesses that you may have noticed if you have seen this movie, except where they relate to the afterlife.

....

Flatliners—What's the Story?

In *Flatliners,* Nelson is a hyper-ambitious medical student who believes he's discovered a way that people can have near-death experiences, get a taste of the afterlife, and come back to life without suffering brain damage. He enlists the help of some of his fellow med students to help in his experiments. While they're wary, their ambition outweighs their skepticism, and at an abandoned museum they plug in their medical equipment and help Nelson "die" and then come back to life. When Nelson returns, he is clearly changed but unable to fully comprehend the experience. The experiment takes an ugly turn when Nelson is visited by a young boy determined to physically attack him. Nelson does not tell his colleagues about the young boy until two more of the group—David and Joe—explore their own afterlives and are forced to confront their own indiscretions. However, unlike the others, Rachel has a slightly different experience, but what they all realize is that to save themselves from what they have wrought, they must find a way to either atone for what they've done or find a way to let go, find peace, and move on.

Common Sense Media
(https://www.commonsensemedia.org/movie-reviews/flatliners-1990)

....

Here are the characters: Nelson is the instigator. It's his idea to flatline. He is wealthy and egotistical. Although he is Dave's friend, he becomes a rival for Rachel's affections.

David Labraccio is an atheist, but he is devoted to human life. As the movie opens, Dave saves a woman's life at the risk of his medical career. He operates on her without permission, because by the time a doctor could have arrived, it would have been too late. Dave is suspended from medical school for four months.

Rachel Manis is intelligent and beautiful. She is caring and warm to the patients in the hospital, but she acts distant and frigid with the male med students.

Joseph Hurley is a pathological womanizer. Even though he has just gotten engaged, Joe tries to pick up girls several times during the film. He has made a practice of secretly videotaping sexual experiences with a long string of girlfriends. He also videotapes sex with his fiancée without her knowledge.

Randall Steckl is kind of an impotent observer. He doesn't have the courage to flatline himself, but his inept observations provide humor.

Defying Death in the Movie *Flatliners*

Nelson convinces Dave, Rachel, Joe, and Randall to help him flatline. He says that his purpose is "to see if there is anything out there beyond death. Philosophy failed. Religion failed. Now it's up to the physical sciences."

After his NDE, Nelson does not describe his experience in detail to the others. He simply says, "There *is* something out there. It's comforting." Shortly after this, when the others leave him alone for a few minutes in the back of Dave's truck, Nelson begins to see strange things. An alley is illumined by an eerie light, and he sees a wounded dog with bandaged legs whimpering and crawling toward him. He says, "Jam?" Then the light vanishes.

That night Nelson dreams the same scene he saw while he was dead, but he hears the sound of a gun and sees some boys running. Then he sees that the boys are really chasing a boy in a hooded sweatshirt. The entire scene becomes black and gray, and he feels himself falling. He screams and wakes up in his own bed. Nelson has opened up the astral plane.

These flatliners have decided to take heaven by force, not in the way that is decreed by God but as they are determined to play God. Declaring that philosophy and religion have failed, they will now go for the god of science and make themselves gods, proving in their own bodies what is life after death, proving that they can die and live again and defy the fates.

Nelson did not go to the etheric plane when he flatlined. He went to the astral plane. And his experience, as we shall see, took place at his point of greatest nonresolution.

At another point in the movie, Nelson is out walking at night through a dark alley. A homeless woman who is talking to herself suddenly turns to him and says, "Right, Nelson? 'Cuz in the end, we all know what we've done." Then the dog appears, and Nelson follows him to a place where he sees the same boy in the hooded sweatshirt that he saw in his dream. The boy attacks Nelson, kicking and punching him repeatedly. The first of a number of physical injuries that Nelson receives from the astral plane is from this incident. He receives more injuries later on.

These are the beginning signs that for Nelson the veil between the physical and astral planes has been pierced. This piercing is a very dangerous thing. You can do it with drugs, and you can do this with Satanic, violent music and various other ways of violating God's energy.

We Brought Our Sins Back

Joe is the next to flatline. Before he does, he calls his fiancée and says, "If anything should ever happen. . . ." When she asks, "What's wrong?" he says, "I don't know. I'm just tired. I'm not making any sense." She is clearly worried about his state of mind.

After Joe is dead, he sees visions from early childhood such as coming through the birth canal, being born, the women who came to admire him as a baby. Then the scene changes to women and girls he has known—flashes of stockinged legs, lips, hands, breasts, eyes, and faces. Then he is revived.

Meanwhile, as Nelson gets increasingly more paranoid, the boy appears to him in his apartment and knocks him out with a hockey stick, adding to Nelson's physical injuries.

Joe also begins to have strange experiences. While talking with a woman about her near-death experience because he feels he needs to share his experience with someone, Joe glances at a TV screen with a football game playing but instead of seeing football he sees a home videotape of himself having sex with a girl. This girl looks at him from the screen and asks, "Why did you do this to me, Joe?" Joe begins to see girls every time he looks at a TV screen. They are all girls he has lied to, and they mouth back to him the lies he has told them.

Dave flatlines next. He first sees flashes of recent events. Then he goes back in time to his earliest memories. Then he is in the womb. Then he sees himself soaring over snow-covered mountains. Suddenly, he hears children chanting on the playground. As the med students start to revive him, he sees an image of a little girl coming toward him.

Dave, too, begins to have strange experiences afterwards. While he is riding on the train he hears a voice say, "Hey, hey, 'Braccio. Got a match? Well, I do." The girl begins to insult him and swear at him. He asks, "Do I know you?" She continues swearing and insulting him while all of the people on the train start laughing at him.

Rachel insists on going next, even though Nelson wanted to go another time first. She says, "I've lost people that are close to me. I just want to make sure they've gone to a good place."

After Rachel is revived and leaves the room, Dave demands that Nelson come clean about his experience. They compare notes. Dave says that he thinks the girl he saw was Winnie Hicks, someone he and others used to gang up on and tease on the playground. Nelson thinks the boy in the hooded sweatshirt that he has been seeing is Billy Mahoney, someone he knew as a kid. Joe reveals his videotaping obsession.

Nelson's interpretation of their experiences is, "We've experienced death. Somehow we brought our sins back physically."

Unconscious and Subconscious Depths

Rachel, who did not hear the accounts that Dave and Nelson exchanged, begins to see visions of her father. When the cadaver she is dissecting appears to come to life and become her father, she screams and runs out of the classroom.

Joe receives retribution for his womanizing when his fiancée, concerned about his phone call, makes a surprise visit while he is not home and discovers his videotape collection. He comes home and sees that he has been exposed. She realizes that he is incapable of having a healthy relationship with a woman. She asks him, "What kind of marriage can we have without trust in it?" She walks out, breaking off their engagement.

Nelson flashes back to his childhood experience with Billy Mahoney. When Nelson was nine years old, he and some other boys chased Billy up a tree. They began pelting him with stones. Billy lost his grip and fell to his death.

Dave looks up Winnie Hicks, who is now a grown woman with a husband, daughter, and home of her own. Nelson had asked to go with Dave because Nelson is afraid to be alone. Nelson waits in the truck while Dave goes into Winnie's house.

Dave tells her that he is sorry for his bullying. At first she brushes off his apology, saying that it's the kind of thing that children do and that it didn't mean anything. But then she reveals through her behavior that it was painful, and in the end she thanks him. Very relieved, Dave thanks her for accepting his apology.

Meanwhile, Nelson begins to feel as if Billy Mahoney is around. He sees a red hood flash by the truck window. He locks the doors. He begins to scream, "Dave, help!" Even though the doors are locked, suddenly Billy appears in the truck and attacks Nelson with an ax-type tool. Nelson picks up a similar one and begins struggling with Billy. Billy's blade moves closer to Nelson's head. It looks as if Nelson will be killed. Billy is pushing down with incredible strength. Then Dave returns to the truck, and Billy disappears. Nelson is holding an ax and struggling with himself.

Back in the city, they all compare notes. Nelson says to Joe and Randall, "Dr. Dave thinks he's solved our karmic problems. Atonement, gentlemen." Dave has atoned for his sin. But Nelson cannot atone for his, since Billy is dead. Nelson tells Joe and Randall the story of his part in Billy's death. Nelson was sent to reform school at age nine.

"I thought I'd paid my dues," Nelson says. "I can still make amends." Then he runs off, jumps into Joe's car, and leaves them stranded.

Meanwhile, Rachel and Dave discuss her seeing her father appear and her sense of being at fault for his death. Dave tells her about his visit with Winnie. "It lifted something. Just asking her for forgiveness," he says. Rachel and Dave sleep together.

Then Dave gets a phone call from Joe and Randall, who were left stranded by Nelson. Dave goes to pick them up, leaving Rachel alone. She enters a kind of dream state and walks into her childhood home, where she finds her father shooting heroin. Nelson calls Dave, but Rachel picks up the phone. Nelson apologizes for getting them into flatlining. He tells her he is going to flatline again, this time alone. He has become desperate.

Psychological Analysis

This is a movie that has many repercussions, certainly tremendous impact on the psyches of those who watch it. It is designed to bring out the unconscious and the subconscious in all of us and make us examine ourselves in depth. So I will now give you the traditional psychological analysis of the main characters.

Through their experiment with death, all four undergo the collapsing of ego boundaries and the infiltration of unresolved childhood experiences into their conscious awareness.

Nelson, the Instigator

Nelson, through his flatlining experience, goes directly back to the point of greatest nonresolution in his subconscious. It replayed because it is demanding attention. Nelson has a morbid preoccupation with death because he is unconsciously preoccupied with resolving his part in the death of Billy Mahoney. Nelson is bound up with intense fear, guilt, and anger. At the unconscious level he is still horrified that Billy was killed partly as a result of his taunting.

Nelson is tormented with guilt but also angry that he had spent years in a reform school and still hasn't "paid his dues." In his successive encounters with Billy Mahoney, the tables are turned on the childhood tragedy. Nelson is now the victim of a viciously angry Billy Mahoney, who appears as the personification of Nelson's own hateful, taunting, murderously aggressive impulses.

The fact that Nelson is physically injured a number of times by Billy shows that Nelson is not only dealing with his own unconscious but also with a collapsing of the astral into the physical plane. Billy Mahoney is a vengeful discarnate. After successive violent encounters with the discarnate Billy Mahoney, each one leaving Nelson with more physical injuries, Nelson becomes terrified and paranoid.

Nelson can no longer distinguish between the conscious and the unconscious, the real and the unreal. He is living more and more in the world of his unconscious death wishes and astral experiences. He is constantly reexperiencing the death scene. Psychologists would refer to this as post-traumatic stress disorder, or PTSD.

After the other medical students confront Nelson and accuse him of not warning them of what they would be facing in their death experiment, Nelson goes into an extreme state. On the one hand, it appears to be complete insanity; on the other, complete accountability. He decides to flatline again in order to make amends by becoming the victim in the original childhood tragedy with Billy Mahoney. In the final retribution scene, both Nelson and Billy are children again. Nelson is the victim of Billy's taunting until Nelson falls from the tree in the death scene. As he falls, Nelson changes from a child to an adult.

This scene symbolizes Nelson's facing the trauma and taking accountability from the level of an adult. When he looks up at the specter of Billy standing over him, Nelson's face has cleared of the fearful, angry, abusive energy. Psychologically he has settled the score with the murderer in his own unconscious and with Billy as the discarnate by killing the "bad" Nelson.

The conflict is resolved, and Nelson is no longer afraid.

He no longer has to torture himself. Billy Mahoney smiles as if to say, "Now you know what it's like," and leaves Nelson once and for all.

Joe, the Womanizer

Joe is unable to have a mature love relationship with a woman. He has an unresolved childhood Oedipus complex. This goes back to a fixation on his childhood relationship with his mother. Joe tries to improve his masculine identity through sexual encounters with women, which he secretly videos for his later viewing. Joe hides his voyeuristic behavior but secretly feels guilty about it.

Joe has split the feminine within. He sees women in two categories: women with whom he can have casual sex, and the woman he truly loves. Jung might say that he has sex with the "witch" and elevates his true love to a "goddess." Joe's retribution comes when his true love discovers his videos, recognizes his basic disrespect for women, and breaks off their relationship.

In his near-death experience, Joe meets a sensual, feminine figure who is dark-haired and looks very much like him. She is his anima, or feminine part, repressed into the unconscious and yet the driving force behind his sexual behavior. By the end of the film, Joe has not made real peace with himself. He still has to resolve his sexual behavior and come to terms with the unconscious anima projection.

Joe's karmic retribution is to lose the woman he really loves. And until he resolves his own feminine side, he will not be likely to have a healthy relationship with a woman. A person like Joe will need therapy to address and resolve the Oedipus complex. He will need to claim his masculine identity and bring his feminine side to conscious awareness and integration with the masculine.

Dave, the Atheist

Dave appears to be the most psychologically whole and most truly caring of the characters in *Flatliners*. He gets involved in the death experiment because he is concerned that the medical students will not be able to bring each other back to life. He goes through the experience himself to try to stop Rachel, whom he loves, from doing it. Dave is healed of his unconscious conflict by facing the wrong he did to Winnie, by asking for forgiveness, and by doing what he can do as an adult to atone for his bullying behavior. His psychological burden is also lifted.

Rachel, the Troubled Child

Rachel's father committed suicide when she was five years old. This age is particularly significant. It is the period labeled by Freud as the "phallic period." This is when the little girl, in the feminine version of the Oedipus complex called the Electra complex, desires to possess her father and therefore feels hostile toward her mother. The healthy resolution comes about when the little girl lets go of her father and identifies with her mother.

Rachel's frigid, distant, and driven manner as an adult woman is the result of her lack of resolution with her father and her unresolved guilt of feeling responsible for his death. For Rachel, her intimate relationship with Dave represents her leaving her father behind and coming into her own as a woman.

In Rachel's final experience with her father, he apologizes and she forgives him. This is called a "corrective emotional experience." By going through the traumatic experience again, she heals her wounded inner child's trauma.

As a child, Rachel didn't realize that her father was shooting heroin. She would not have remembered that part of the scene because it would have made her father responsible for his own death. Her mother's reaction to his suicide had convinced Rachel that it was Rachel's fault. Psychologically, she could not remember that her father was shooting heroin until she was ready to face resolution as an adult.

Forgiveness, Karma, and Resolution

So the chief positive benefit of the self-induced NDEs was that three of the four students achieved a kind of resolution and were able to go on with their lives. But they still had to balance their karma.

Let's examine what the movie says about forgiveness, karma, and resolution. The movie is accurate in its statement that we must atone for our sins and balance our karma. It is inaccurate in its statement of how we atone. Three people apologize in this movie. Dave apologizes to Winnie and she forgives him. Nelson apologizes to Billy and he forgives him. Rachel's father apologizes to her and she forgives him.

What remains in the psyches of Nelson, Dave, and Rachel's father after the apology is the propensity to inflict pain on others. What remains in the victims Billy, Winnie, and Rachel are the psychological scars of the experience. When Dave apologizes to Winnie, she acknowledges that she was hurt by the playground teasing and thanks him for coming. He walks away. Where does that leave her? Are the scars in her psyche resolved? Is she now going to be a different adult woman?

Winnie's forgiveness of Dave was the beginning. It didn't necessarily heal Dave of the propensity to be cruel. And it didn't heal Winnie of the scars and the pain of being taunted on the playground that were there in her inner child of the past, "the ugly little girl" whom she said she hadn't thought of in years.

Forgiveness is indeed the beginning of resolution, but it is not the ending. Forgiveness is a very necessary step. But in fact, it is considered to be the second step on the spiritual path. Accepting the will of God in your life is the first step.

The second step is to forgive—your friends, your enemies, and all who have ever wronged you—and to ask for forgiveness for all wrongs you have ever committed. Forgiveness means that something is lifted, as Dave shares in the movie. And what is lifted is some percentage of the weight of karma. The burden of the act itself is carried by God.

With the grace of this intercession, the third step on the path of resolution is that we can go out and render service to life that will balance that karma. Otherwise we would be so bowed down with the full weight of our karma that we could hardly do anything.

We can pray for those who have been psychologically bruised by our actions and call for healing. If we know who they are, we can help them. If we can't balance the karma in one life because our actions have affected masses of people, we may reincarnate a number of times to balance karma that we have made with society in general. This is why reincarnation is the mercy of God.

Rachel's forgiveness of her father is absolutely essential. Forgiveness is a step toward resolution in any karmic equation. But from that point on, Rachel will have to deal with the problems in her psychology that I already discussed.

Forgiveness starts the spiral of a healing process. Rachel's father said that he was sorry. But how many addicts have we seen say they're sorry, promise to quit, and never have the will or the guts to do it. His ultimate forgiveness of himself, by himself, will come when he integrates his personality in God through his Higher Self. He must understand and accept that he needs divine intercession, that he cannot pull himself up by his own bootstraps. He is wrestling with the forces of death and hell. He needs a divine mediator.

The Karma of Drugs

Rachel's father is not free of the heroin addiction simply because he is dead. His emotions and mind will still crave the experience of shooting heroin. Even without a body, he may go about hooking into the energies of other heroin addicts who are still in physical embodiment. As I told you earlier, in order to experience vicarious enjoyment of the drug rush or drug high, discarnates such as Rachel's father may hook into those who have addictions and still have a body.

Rachel's father will bring his vulnerability to heroin addiction back with him when and if he reincarnates. He will have to confront heroin and say no to it. He will have to have his victory over heroin before he can experience that full sense of atonement and that full integration with God. Asking for forgiveness is an important step in balancing karma, but after that we must balance the debt through service to life and deliver ourselves of the psychological propensity to make more of the same karma.

There is a record in the soul, in the psyche, in the subconscious. It is the point of our vulnerability. Therefore we reincarnate in order to be strengthened. And we find that our strength is in our Higher Self.

The Karma of Murder

Now let's take a look at what the movie says about balancing the karma of murder. Nelson does not achieve resolution until he is put in Billy's place and experiences the same death he inflicted on Billy. Nelson is pelted with stones, loses his grip, and falls from the tree.

The truth is that karma is not balanced if "I hit you and you hit me back—Now we're even." If I murdered you in a past life and you murder me now, we do not both get away scot-free. The act of murder is a violation of cosmic law. The act of releasing pent up emotion in physical violence—of hitting someone or beating someone up—is a violation of the law of love. It is cosmos itself that is knocked out of its course, so to speak, by the injuries of life against life.

The law of karma is not a law of vengeance. Atonement for a deed is not just an eye for an eye and a tooth for a tooth, but the restoration of that which is lost. If you murder someone, you must give birth to someone.

Our children are usually the children of our karma—both positive and negative karma. People come together because they both owe a certain individual karma or because a certain individual owes them karma. Or they may have karma with each other and with different children. One child might be the wife's karma and the other child might be the husband's karma, good or bad karma. And people realize this. We often hear people say things such as, "She's her father's child."

So the karma for murder is always to give life in return. The karma for violence is to give peace and comfort and consolation and support, and to overcome the emotional or psychological tendency to control others through violence.

Another karma for murder may be to die inopportunely in one's next life. Through accidental death, we not only experience death but we find that our opportunity to balance karma and to fulfill our reason for being is cut off—often in the prime of life.

Every situation of karma is different. It is certainly true that in some cases the death penalty, or the corresponding act of murder for murder, may balance most or all of that karma. Since karma is so complex between two people and it goes back for so many lifetimes, it is therefore possible that the eye-for-an-eye or the tooth-for-a-tooth law would apply in some cases. But even if it does apply, it does not count for the resolution of the karmic records and of the psychology.

Beyond Punishment and Forgiveness

A murderer being required to go through therapy or to go to prison to come to terms with human concepts of love and compassion is only a temporary fix at best. Human love is a necessary ingredient in our human lives. But permanent healing, transformation, and transmutation can only come through divine love and divine intercession.

What does Nelson have to do to balance his karma for his part in the death of Billy Mahoney? Going to reform school is not the whole of it. It does not restore Billy's life nor does it take from Billy the tremendous burden of hatred that the children put on him in their taunting. The real pain Billy will carry until he achieves psychological resolution is the pain of rejection by his peers. There is nothing more painful to a child. Billy will have to work hard, very hard, to consume that hatred by love. Nelson's sufferings do not alleviate the sufferings of Billy. In order to atone for his deed, Nelson has to do more than suffer.

Also, Nelson must do something to make it possible for Billy to once again breathe the breath of life and to be delivered of the burden of the experience and its trauma—first of all, the burden of being hated by all of his playmates, and second, the burden of this untimely death that cut off his life at such a young age. It may have been Billy's karma to die by stoning and the fall from the tree. Or he may have been an innocent victim.

There are always new acts of karma where an innocent person is wronged. New karma is being made every day. But since we've been evolving on this planet in some cases for millions of years, there are a lot of accounts to settle. And it is surfacing today. Today, you can almost be guaranteed that what is going on in your life is a karmic situation. And if it's not karmic, it certainly is soul testing on the spiritual path.

Physical Harm from Discarnates

The question arises: Was Billy Mahoney real or a figment of Nelson's mind? The answer is that he was both. This is why Billy could inflict physical harm on Nelson, but it is also why Billy disappeared when Dave came upon their violent encounter in the truck.

Nelson has a vivid recollection of Billy Mahoney in the tree and can recall it at any time, and he does so because the trauma remains unresolved. Billy of course also has intense emotions tied up in the situation. He had acute anger as well as fear at the time that he was being stoned, but this became a rage as he fell to his death. He could not vent this rage on his playmates because he was dead. Therefore, later on in the events with Nelson, Billy at some level of his being went out apart from his conscious mind—through his unconscious and subconscious records—in an attempt to work vengeance.

When Nelson punctured the veil between the physical world and the world beyond, he became a magnet that attracted to himself the hostile emotions of Billy Mahoney. And so that identity as an objective reality was able to contact Nelson. Even before this, Billy was already bombarding Nelson with anger, even though Nelson couldn't identify its source. You may be surprised that I am saying that Billy Mahoney was still bombarding him with anger after so many years. Billy may have forgiven Nelson on one level, but on another level he was attacking Nelson.

Forces from the other side can break through into our physical world and cause physical injury. The case of Nelson being physically injured by Billy from the astral plane is an extreme example that rarely happens. African witch doctors and voodoo practitioners can cause things like this to happen. Human hatred can cause deaths and accidents on the other side of the planet. But have you ever heard someone say, "I was walking down the stairs and all of a sudden—for no reason at all—my feet came out from under me and I broke my leg"? You too may have experienced some kind of strange mishap where there was no apparent cause.

Knowing that this can happen does not have to make us apprehensive or superstitious. It tells us that we have to guard our consciousness so that we don't have vulnerabilities to the projectiles of other people's thought and feeling worlds. Archangel Michael will protect us when we ask him to.

Playing God

Nelson decides that he will put himself through the death experience to atone. He thinks he will finally be free from the attacks of his own unconscious mind and Billy's unconscious mind. But if Nelson had succeeded in permanently killing himself, he still would have had karma with Billy.

This is where so-called modern man (which is really the reincarnation of those from an ancient civilization of a technologically advanced people who destroyed their world) plays God. Modern man wants to call the shots. He wants to make the rules and say, "OK, I did this act. Now I'm going to do this good thing. And by doing this good thing I'm going to wipe this debt out."

The big element that is missing in this movie is the Divine Mediator (your Higher Self or Christ Self). I see no humility in the characters of *Flatliners*. I see the suffering and pangs of their anguish, but I see no divine lubricant between themselves and their deeds. When they discover that they must reckon with karmic consequences, they decide that they will call the shots. They are attempting to circumvent God and the Divine Mediator.

The flatliners are thieves and robbers because they are robbing the grave of its due. In due course we shall arrive at the portals of life and death. We will have our life review, and we will face all those things that we have failed to balance in this life. When people ask me for advice in this matter, I tell them that my advice is to make your peace with God, with every part of life that you have ever wronged, and with every part of life that has ever wronged you.

When you submit to the will of God—when you can surrender your human will to the divine will—then you have truly begun the spiritual path. When you desire to return home to God, to play the game of life according to his rules and not your rules, then you have the humility of heart that allows the Christ to enter in.

Science versus Religion

I would like to further examine what *Flatliners* says about Jesus, who is that Christ. The painting of Jesus hanging on the wall of Rachel's childhood home is an indelible part of the memory of her father's death. In fact, her near-death experience begins with this picture.

The choice to use this painting may show a subconscious

anger against Jesus by the creator of the film. The movie's message is, "Jesus didn't help her, did he? He was a painting on the wall. He didn't stop her father from killing himself. If Jesus were a real savior, he wouldn't allow such things to happen." The message to the audience is that religion is a sham. Jesus isn't going to save you in your hour of need, so you have to save yourself. The presence of the painting expresses resentment towards religion probably stemming from lifetimes of bad experiences with organized religion on the part of whoever inserted this.

Another character in *Flatliners* who wants to play God is Dave. After he fails to revive Nelson, Dave yells out to the universe, "I'm sorry, guys. I'm sorry we stepped on your f**g territory. I'm sorry. Isn't that enough?" I am not even sure who he's talking to. I am not even sure that the "guys" aren't the fallen ones for whom science is god. And the students have stepped on the territory of these gods rather than the Almighty.

This scene is the most painful experience for me in the entire movie because it shows the profane relationship of Dave's soul to the compassionate God who ensouls the universe. "Isn't that enough?" is the telltale line. It's all on Dave's terms. He should be forgiven because he says he's sorry. That's supposed to be enough. He will take no accountability for taking heaven by force.

Free Will and Accountability

Dave's sense that Nelson doesn't deserve to die may or may not be accurate, but it's Dave's assessment. He excuses Nelson's childhood participation in Billy's death and says it was a mistake because Nelson was a little kid. But Nelson and the other kids on the playground committed acts of adults. Dave is preaching a sermon of nonaccountability to God. But God's universe runs on accountability.

If the story were true to life, we could conclude that Dave was right. Nelson didn't deserve to die, but not for Dave's reasons. Nelson does come back to life, and the audience is relieved. Dave sees himself as a savior because he decides to try again to bring Nelson to life even though everyone else has given up. Dave becomes a Christlike figure, but he doesn't get God's permission to save Nelson or think that he has to obey God's rules.

So Dave cries out to the universe for help. He, as a self-styled god, is about to lose in the experiment. And when he brings Nelson back, he certainly is not about to give God the glory. The only character to thank God is Randall Steckl, the so-called jerk. This is telling us that only jerks say things like that. True heroes stand and fall on their own actions.

Free will is the gift of God for self-determination. In the name of the god of science, the flatliners are rebelling against God's law and gift of free will. When you exercise your free will on earth in order to bring forth the patterns God made in the heavens so that you can return to the heavenly abode, then you are using your free will in the way it was meant to be used.

In order for you to exercise free will, God had to give you an alternative. He had to allow darkness. He had to allow you to mingle with fallen angels. Otherwise you would not be able to exercise your free will to choose the right, to choose the light. God gave us free will so that we would not become computerized extensions of his mind. Our choice for light or darkness would prove to God that we are not choosing him because his offering is better, although indeed it is. We are choosing him because we *love* him more than the greatest titillations that the nightside of life can offer us.

The Price of Soul Freedom

Some people are angry with God because he allows earthquakes and death and accidents. They want a fanciful God who will do everything for them. But this would deny his grand experiment of free will, which includes dealing with the results of our exercise of free will—karma.

The name of the game is freedom. People want freedom without paying the price for it. They want the state to take care of them, they want socialism, they want communism. They want more and more governmental controls. They don't want to be co-creators with God. They don't want to be accountable for their actions or for their fate. They want to make the government or somebody else accountable so that they have somebody else to blame for their misfortunes.

I believe much of this psychology is inculcated in childhood through erroneous religious concepts, through indulgent parents who do not make their children come to grips with reality and deal with problems on a day-to-day basis. They do not teach their children that life involves problem solving, that life has consequences, and that we have to have the guts to deal with the consequences of our actions and to pay the price. Extending love and forgiveness is not paying the price, but it's the very important beginning of the karmic resolution. Now we must go forth to pay our debts to one another, to God, and to society.

One book that I recommend for a deeper look at this psychology is *The Undiscovered Self,* by Carl Jung. I have a great respect for Jung, and I feel he was inspired by the ascended masters. He wrote this book in the 1950s as a commentary on what was happening in the conflict between communism and the free world—the empowering of the state, the state becoming all-powerful, and what this does to the individual, how the individual is destroyed. So you can study this from the level of your Higher Self and not from the fascination of the human mind with itself, which is a very dangerous thing.*

Conclusion

Coming back to the movie *Flatliners,* my assessment is that these four med students went to the astral plane because of their nonresolution. If they had not been revived, they would have been stuck in those scenes. They would have been stuck until angels were called forth by those who would take the time and make the calls to free them.

My service to life includes making calls for souls of light at the hour of their transition, including those who for some reason have gotten stuck in the astral plane. Archangel Michael is always ready to use his sword of blue flame to help those who have passed on reach the highest level of the afterlife that their karma allows.

This is just a brief assessment of the movie *Flatliners.* The movie unfolds nuance after nuance. You may not know where to begin or end interpreting it—until, of course, you remember that it's only fiction. But the spiritual issues in our lives are very real.

---

*Carl G. Jung had an unusual near-death experience in 1944, which you can read about in his autobiographical account on page 215, Appendix C.

CHAPTER 6

Commanding the Light

*We have to pray with power and energy
because the forces of the astral plane
are unleashed in the physical world today.*

ELIZABETH CLARE PROPHET

You can see that you need to be very aware and protect yourself from the situations I've described for you concerning the dangers of discarnates. I want you to have the spiritual tools that will help you to master and protect yourself so that you can fulfill your purpose in this life and move on to higher levels.

The method the ascended masters have given us to accomplish divesting ourselves of these lower vibrations and entering into etheric levels has to do with dynamic decrees, the use of the science of the spoken Word. I use the word *dynamic* because decrees are powerful. They invoke a lot of energy—energy that is disciplined and focused, energy that fills a matrix of words with light to manifest in us that which is desired.

Decrees are a powerful method of accessing the power of God that is already inside of you and of expanding your divine potential, which is also right inside of you. Decrees are a form of spoken prayer, as are Hindu and Buddhist mantras and forms of spoken prayer from other cultural traditions that have been passed down through the ages. Jesus used spoken prayer in his healing when he commanded the sick to be healed and foul spirits to be expelled. Decreeing connects you with your Higher Self, who releases a tremendous amount of spiritual power and energy to you.

Here is a simple decree:

Let the light expand in the center of my heart!

That is a command, and the light will obey it. Simple calls like this help you to focus so that all of the light goes into the center of your heart. Try saying it and see how you will feel a response from your Higher Self.

Fervor of Heart and Mind

A simple call made with a fervent heart, made with great God-desire and the knowledge that God's law is unerring, works. This kind of call always compels the answer. We just need to remember that the right change can be produced without our conscious knowledge of what this change ought to be.

One of the ascended masters told us,

> If your call is a weak little call, halfhearted, you will get a weak little answer, halfhearted.
>
> But if, with all the fervor of your heart and mind and being, you cry out to God . . . on behalf of those who are suffering in the earth, and you offer powerful invocations, . . . if you do this daily . . . you will establish such a tie with the heart of the Godhead that no lawful prayer you offer for the rest of your life will be denied you![1]

We have to pray with power and energy because the forces of the astral plane are unleashed in the physical world today. To deal with them and to deal with demon possession and the burdens that are upon people, you have to speak with the authority that God gave us when he said, "Command ye me."² So when you commune in purity with your Higher Self and speak a decree such as the ones I am giving you, you give it as a command, with tremendous power.

That commanding God Presence, that tremendous power, comes through your Higher Self, who is with you, who decrees through you. Believe me, it is necessary to pray in this powerful manner to extricate yourself from the lower pulls of the astral plane. And I hope that you will come to enjoy the process.

No matter what spiritual path you follow, you can benefit from adding decrees to your devotions because dynamic decrees are the most powerful of all applications to God.

Sealed in White Light

You can protect yourself from all kinds of harm, not merely physical but also that which is unseen, by invoking a cylinder of white light that I call the tube of light. You can put it on first thing in the morning and reinforce it throughout the day. Try giving this call with heartfelt intensity:

Beloved I AM Presence bright
Round me seal your tube of light
From ascended master flame
Called forth now in God's own name.
Let it keep my temple free
From all discord sent to me.

I AM calling forth violet fire
To blaze and transmute all desire,
Keeping on in freedom's name
*Till I AM one with the violet flame.**

Keep yourself protected. And if for any reason you feel inharmonious, reestablish your harmony and reestablish your tube of light. Negative forces can create circumstances in your life that are calculated to disturb you until you lose your balance and become discordant, which causes a loss of light.

God will not give to you any more light than you can keep in harmony. If you can keep your harmony, then you can increase your light. If you are incapable of keeping your harmony, along come invisible forces that create a problem in your world, and you get all upset. Out goes the light you received from God, and you are depleted.

This is why you need the reinforcement of the tube of light—because you cannot be harmonious by your human will. You need your Higher Self and the angels with you. There are many things that we cannot do by human willpower. We can be overcome by habit patterns, even from past lives, of being upset and getting disturbed over things. Seeking the higher way of oneness with God is the way to begin to develop the strength to resist falling back into those patterns.

I'd like to tell you an amazing story about someone who used this tube of light decree regularly and devotedly. A man from an African nation told me about this event in his life. He had served in his country's government. After the government fell, he was imprisoned with others who had also served in the government.

---

*See "The Miracle of the Violet Flame" on page 134 for more about the violet flame and what it does.

While he was in prison, someone introduced him to decrees. He said them over and over again through the day and through the night. They were his constant comfort.

One day, after many weeks in prison, he and the other prisoners were called before a firing squad. They were all lined up, and the command to fire was given. Everyone fell but this man. The soldiers looked at him, and they looked at him again in disbelief. The command was given once more, and this time they all trained on this man and fired again. Still he didn't fall.

Then the soldiers had great fear. The head soldier said, "You must be a good man. We'll let you go."

The man lived to tell me this story, and he said that it was his "tube of light" that saved him.

You Need an Advocate

Always and always and always, the way to begin to deal with malevolent spirits, demons, or discarnates is through the call to Archangel Michael. He is the defender of our faith, our persons, our families, our communities, our nations. The reason that you don't challenge forces of darkness on your own is that in most cases they will have greater attainment through the misuse of God's light, energy, and consciousness than you will have attainment in the qualification of God's light, energy, and consciousness.

Therefore you need an advocate before the Father. God gave to us a Higher Self, a Christ Self. If you are going to cast out demons, you always cast them out saying: *"In the name of Almighty God and my own Holy Christ Self, in the name of Archangel Michael, I cast out this discarnate entity."*

However before you make this call, you need to call forth the assistance of Archangel Michael and his sword of blue flame.

You and I are no direct match for this darkness. But Archangel Michael is. At our call, he will take his flaming sword of the Spirit and sweep it right through us to clear conditions affecting our physical bodies as well as our astral, mental, and even etheric bodies, removing as much as God's law will allow. He also aligns us with the unique inner blueprint that God gave to each one of us. But we must reinforce this action daily with our devotions because the light of the angels tends to rise and return to etheric levels unless drawn down on a daily basis to the level where we dwell.

The principle of giving decrees and of giving invocations is that there are heavenly hosts and armies of the Lord who will come to our defense. They answer our call.

Daily Protection

It's a good idea to carve out at least twenty minutes after rising in the morning to devote to your protection decrees for the day. You can even decree while you shower or during your commute to work. Just do it! Always call forth your tube of light first, then the blue flame of protection.

The following is a call that you can give at any moment of the day or night when you feel the need to establish your protection. Visualize Archangel Michael being accompanied by limitless numbers of angels who will protect and escort you wherever you go. He will also seal those who have passed on and keep them out of the astral plane.

Lord Michael before, Lord Michael behind,
Lord Michael to the right, Lord Michael to the left,
Lord Michael above, Lord Michael below,
Lord Michael, Lord Michael wherever I go!

I AM his love protecting here!
I AM his love protecting here!
I AM his love protecting here!

Guard, guard, guard us
  By the lightning of thy love!
Guard, guard, guard us
  By thy Great Self above!
Guard, guard, guard us
  By thy secret power of light!
Guard, guard, guard us
  By thy great and glorious might!
And seal us safe forever
  In thy diamond heart of light!

See Archangel Michael directing the power of his flaming sword to consume the cause and core of all negative conditions, including those stemming from demons or discarnate entities that may be within or upon you or upon your loved ones.

Three Words and a Safe Landing

I had just recently learned about decrees, and prior to this moment, I had not yet ever given a decree. This was my introduction to Archangel Michael.

I boarded a Boeing 737 plane for my weekly commute and sat near the back in my usual window seat. Fifteen minutes into the flight there was a loud pop. The notes that I was working on flew out of my hands.

Without thinking, I called out, "Mighty I AM!" I immediately dropped my head to my knees and waited for the flight attendant to make the standard emergency announcement.

Then I looked up and saw blue sky. The entire top of the

front third of the plane was gone from behind the cockpit back to the wing and from the floorboard on one side of the plane to the floorboard on the other side.

There was no one to make the safety announcement. One flight attendant had been sucked out of the plane when the fuselage peeled away. Another flight attendant was vainly trying to pull oxygen masks from what remained of the sagging overhead compartments.

I had no idea whether anyone was flying the plane, and I thought to myself, "So this is what it's like to die." Then I realized that I wasn't afraid. In fact, a sense of peace seemed to pervade the entire plane.

I still didn't know if we had a flight crew but we seemed to be on course. We were at 14,000 feet with a good portion of the plane gone as we cruised at 345 miles per hour.

But we did land safely, thirteen minutes later at the airport —thanks to the skill of a well-trained pilot with Archangel Michael at his side! Everyone involved in the National Transportation Safety Board's investigation declared it a miracle that the plane had held together that long and that the flight attendant was the only fatality.   A witness to Archangel Michael

National Transportation Safety Board (NTSB)

What Is behind Violence?

Another kind of entity besides a discarnate entity is a mass entity. Mass entities are forcefields of humanly misqualified energy. They are the thought and feeling creations of unascended man. These entities are the accumulation of humanity's own momentums of hatred, violence, war, greed, mayhem, murder, gossip, and so forth. These entities float on the astral plane as islands of darkness. They can be as large as a city, and they are very deadly. They come upon people whose bodies and whose minds they can use to wreak havoc.[3]

Diabolical forces direct these pockets of darkness against unsuspecting souls. Acts of crime diagnosed as temporary insanity are sometimes brought about when vortices of vicious energy are focused upon the auric fields of unsuspecting people who lack a defense against such forces or of people who have made themselves susceptible through their own negativity.

This is why sometimes when there are mass murders, shootings, or other violent acts you see a repeat of them. They come in waves and cycles, and they sweep the country. Unbalanced individuals hear about a mass murder in the news. They get totally absorbed in it in a crazed way. That mass entity gravitates toward them by the principle of like attracts like. And that mass of demons is like a swarm of bees. It's a huge energetic forcefield that moves toward the weakest link in the human chain and acts through that person.[4] Mass entities can work through madmen, through leaders, through people who direct all types of murders and atrocities on a large scale.

Now you can see why the best efforts of our police, security forces, and military have not been able to stop growing levels of violence and crime. Their efforts must be supported by spiritual work on astral darkness, on the powers behind the physical appearances. Our calls to Archangel Michael are necessary to stop these astral accumulations from entering and remaining in our own subconscious as well as in the subconscious of unsuspecting, vulnerable, and especially unstable people across the world.

I remember an incident in a major city from years ago when a killer had committed fourteen murders and twenty rapes during seven months. A woman told me that at five a.m. one morning she felt in her heart the intense determination that this was the day the killer had to be caught. She started praying to Archangel Michael and repeated her prayers by the hour, dedicating it to one purpose—the catching of this killer. He was caught that very day.

This story shows how Archangel Michael can intercede through the prayers of one faithful soul. You may not believe that such a feat could be accomplished through the prayers of one individual. Miracles are for believers. But you will become a believer when you start seeing the miracles that Archangel Michael performs through your prayers.[5]

Paper Tigers Can Harm

In one of Raymond Moody's books, he tells of a young man who attempted suicide. The man "described images of some horrific beings clutching and clawing at him. It was something like descending into Dante's Inferno."[6] So are these horrific beings in the astral plane real or imagined?

An ascended master explained this to us: "Let me stress to you that a thought is real. Let me stress to you that an idea in picturization is real, that when individuals see a dragon of darkness while in a trip into the astral world by the use of psychedelic drugs, they are experiencing a horrendous meeting with a very vicious and destructive dark force. . . ." But he also stressed that these images are paper tigers compared to the power wielded by Archangel Michael.[7]

What, then, do you think would be the impact of many thousands of people putting their attention on the astral images of horror movies, images purveyed on the Internet, or even of annual Halloween activities?[8] Another master told us that from television programs and movies, our minds receive "millions of impressions of negativity, which are then processed and assimilated in the subconscious mind." In fact, he said, "The media is the primary controlling factor that manipulates the minds of the youth in America and the world. And you had better realize that although the content of some movies is extremely violent, it is also subtle."[9]

....

Archangel Michael's Appearance

I remember having a vivid and terrifying nightmare. I was forcibly locked up in a deep cave. There were demons all around tormenting and torturing me, while on the other side of a wall of prison bars I could see my body sleeping. I was crying out and pleading to my body to wake up, but to no avail. Finally in desperation I remembered the simple call to Archangel Michael.

Instantly I was back in my body. As I sat up in my bed, the fear began to subside. A blur of blue angels was rapidly pursuing a shadowy mass that soon left through the open window and disappeared from sight followed closely by the angelic pursuers.

Redirecting my gaze to the foot of my bed, I then saw Archangel Michael standing there, his golden hair wafting in solar breezes from another dimension. Filling the entire space from floor to ceiling, he held his sword before him. He had the angular, youthful face of a warrior and brilliant golden armor and heavenly wings—all radiating and interpenetrated with transparent, vibrant, cobalt blue.

If a man's eyes are windows to his soul, then an archangel's eyes are portals to the entire cosmos, past, present, and future. In his gaze I felt comfort, peace, and transcendent love. No harm could ever come to me with Michael as my guardian.   A grateful devotee

A Powerful Call for Heaven's Help

I want to introduce you to a prayer to Archangel Michael that was written down by Pope Leo XIII after he saw a powerful vision of threatening evil. This prayer was said at the conclusion of the Catholic Mass from 1886 to 1964. Catholics use it to exorcise evil spirits that prey upon one's light and consciousness and to clear forces of darkness from the earth.[10]

I have taken this prayer and added some lines that are essential to us in our understanding of the spiritual equation today. I have also added a place for you to insert your own specific prayers for the binding of dark forces attacking your household or for any situation in your life where you believe that there are forces that may be moving against you, your community, nation, or the entire earth. These situations include possessing discarnate entities and demons that cause our youth to be addicted to drugs and to all kinds of harmful substances and activities. There is no question that these entities enter our children and remain there, causing a change of personality and a point of rebellion.

Before giving you my version of the prayer to Archangel Michael, I want to make this invocation for you:

> *In the name of the light of God that never fails, I call to the Lord God Almighty. Mighty I AM Presence, Holy Christ Self, Archangel Michael, and legions of white fire and blue lightning, we call to you in this hour for the binding of every discarnate entity and demon that may be affecting our individual lives, the lives of our families, our spouses, our children. We demand the binding in this hour of those causes and conditions which afflict us and the entire planetary body.*
>
> *Blessed Mother Mary, all saints of heaven from East and West, hear our prayers on behalf of all those who need support in this hour. We thank thee and accept it done this hour in full power. In the name of the Father, the Son, the Holy Spirit, and the Divine Mother, Amen.*

You can give the following prayer once, three times, nine times, or until you feel that the action of the light is accomplished for your intentions:

> *Saint Michael the Archangel, defend us in Armageddon, be our protection against the wickedness and snares of the devil; may God rebuke him, we humbly pray; and do thou, O Prince of the heavenly host, by the power of God, bind the forces of Death and Hell, the seed of Satan, the false hierarchy of Antichrist, and all evil spirits who wander through the world for the ruin of souls, and remand them to the Court of the Sacred Fire for their final judgment, including:*
>
> [Give your personal prayers here.]
>
> *Cast out the dark ones and their darkness, the evildoers and their evil words and works, cause, effect, record, and memory, into the lake of sacred fire prepared for the devil and his angels.*[11]
>
> *In the name of the Father, the Son, the Holy Spirit, and the Mother, Amen.*

The Miracle of the Violet Flame

Beyond calling to Archangel Michael, what do you need to do about the kinds of situations that I have described? After the blue-lightning angels have cleared the discarnates, demons, and every kind of negative force in your world, it's time to fill the vacant space that has been left with violet flame. In fact, the essential key to balancing karma on an individual and on a world scale is the violet flame.

The violet flame combines the blue flame of God's power with the pink flame of God's love to become a universal solvent of mercy, transmutation, and forgiveness. It erases karma. Ongoing use of the violet flame can transmute the accumulation of humanity's negative karma of many incarnations over the centuries that not only gives the world a sense of heaviness but if unchecked could bring greater darkness upon the earth.*

When we invoke this flame of God's forgiveness, these dark accumulations burst aflame. We can visualize ourselves, our loved ones, the political scene, the economy, our nation, international relations, and every unfortunate manifestation within this conflagration of mercy's flame, filling the world with joyous, leaping waves of violet flame and forgiveness. You can use the violet flame to liberate the very atoms, cells, and electrons of every level of your heaven and your earth. Here is a meditation to help you feel the action of the violet flame:

Let the energies that you have locked in human habit patterns of misunderstanding be unlocked by the divine habit pattern of understanding God's laws governing our use of the sacred fire. Let the energy that is captive to the human will now be captive to the divine will.

Let these energies come forth in obedience to the grand design which we now invoke as the blueprint for our earth and her evolutions. "As Above, so below," through the science of the spoken Word, from the beginning of "Let there be light!" unto the ending "And there was light!"

The violet flame does not destroy, for God's law is precise: God's energy is neither created nor destroyed. The violet flame changes, transforms. It strips atoms and molecules of the dense overlay of human imperfection. The natural divine perfection of the soul and her original

---

*For a meditation on the violet flame with mantras given along with harp music, go to https://www.youtube.com/watch?v=3mVOKzv2eYQ.

desire to be whole is restored. The encrustations of illusion and the delusions of the pseudo self, and even the laws of old age and death are dissolved.

The violet flame is the elixir of life, the fountain of youth, the laughter of angels. Its buoyant strength and zestful joy make mockery of the astral levels of hell. In the wake of the all-consuming conflagration of the violet flame of the Holy Spirit, all that is left is the real in you and in God!

Being the Instrument of God

The decree I will give you now uses the name of God, "I AM," with a series of affirmations of this sacred fire that is the violet flame. Always keep in mind that when we say, "I AM," we are affirming that "God in me is."

So when we say, "I AM the violet flame in action in me now," we are saying, "God in me is the violet flame in action in me now." It is a very interesting law of forcefields. We are declaring that where I AM, there God is. And where God is, he is the fullness of this action, this specific action of the violet flame, which is his very own being.

It takes, then, understanding of the Law and meditation upon God's very own being to make our use of the science of the spoken Word effective. We are not absently or vainly repeating words when we give decrees. We are entering into a very sacred science whereby we voluntarily enter into a oneness with God, becoming a co-creator with him. The mediator of this co-creation is always our Higher Self, or Holy Christ Self.

Visualize a threefold flame of God's power, wisdom, and love expanding from within your heart—the blue plume of God's power to the left, the yellow plume of God's wisdom in the center, and the pink plume of God's love to the right.

Now see a sphere of white light around your threefold flame. Give this decree aloud until you feel the action of the violet flame flowing through you. Then see it expand as a great sphere of cosmic consciousness.

I AM the violet flame
In action in me now
I AM the violet flame
To light alone I bow
I AM the violet flame
In mighty cosmic power
I AM the light of God
Shining every hour
I AM the violet flame
Blazing like a sun
I AM God's sacred power
Freeing everyone

In full faith I thankfully accept this manifest right here and now with full power, eternally sustained, all-powerfully active, ever expanding, and world enfolding!

When I give a decree, it is with a voice that is different from my speaking voice. It is God in me speaking from the very depths of my heart and my soul. When I open my mouth and center my energies in the heart, I am totally surrendering my being to God. This centering allows the energy of the Holy Spirit to use my throat chakra, or energy center. And the same will happen for you as you become comfortable with the understanding of being the instrument of God.

CHAPTER 7

Reincarnation—What You Need to Know

Genius is experience.
Some seem to think that it is a gift or talent,
but it is the fruit of long experience in many lives.
Some are older souls than others, and so they know more. . . .
I would like to communicate to others the calmness
that the long view of life gives to us.

HENRY FORD

Western religions, apart from their mystical traditions, are the only ones to conclude that the soul has only one life on earth. Yet the number of Americans, including many Christians, who believe in reincarnation has been steadily rising over the years. Many more are curious about it.

Scientists say that they do not know how to measure or study reincarnation. How do you put a trace on a soul? Nevertheless, a growing number of doctors and scientists are becoming convinced that there is something—a higher intelligence, a spiritual energy—that directs affairs in the body and disengages from it upon death. It may be that scientists will one day be able to measure and track the path of this energy (call it the soul or consciousness if you will) from one body to the next.

The differences between a near-death experience and reincarnation are slight. After an NDE, you go back into the same body that you were in before. When you reincarnate, you get a new body. In an NDE, the time you spend on the other side is usually short, while the time between incarnations is typically longer. After an NDE, people seem to vividly remember the experience. Recollections of past incarnations, on the other hand, are rare and tend to be fuzzy.

In October 2018, the Pew Research Center wrote that 33 percent of all U.S. adults they surveyed in December 2017 believe in reincarnation. Certain subsets registered higher, such as Catholics at 36 percent; and some were lower, such as evangelicals at 19 percent. A subset of "religiously unaffiliated" people who reported that their religion is "nothing in particular" came in at 51 percent.[1]

The increase in NDEs, out-of-body experiences, and past-life recollections has contributed to the rise in the belief in reincarnation. Some stories of past-life recollections are imprecise and unverifiable, and some are flat-out wrong, a mixture of fantasy and fiction. Other accounts, however, are eerie in their accuracy. Some people dismiss the belief in reincarnation as wishful thinking or escapism. While it can become that, it can also be a powerful tool for spiritual development.

Reincarnation tells us that life is a continuum. It tells us that what we did in our past lives affects our current life. Understanding this can help us to overcome phobias, chronic health problems, difficulties in relationships, and even personality traits that undermine us in our careers and family life. When we take accountability for our own doings, good and bad, we are in the driver's seat.

Think how different it would be if we were taught in Western civilization to understand reincarnation. We would know that our present suffering is often caused by our past actions—not our parents, not our spouse or children, not society.

Reincarnation and Christianity

Most Christian churches would tell you that you cannot believe in reincarnation and still be a Christian. Without reincarnation, it's only one life, and you either go to heaven or to hell. In reality, most of us aren't ready for heaven, but we're not bad enough to go to any place like hell.

Don't you find it odd that in the modern world others should tell us what to believe or not believe? It's amazing to me that people allow someone else to dictate to them what is the reality of their innermost being.

I know that Jesus did teach reincarnation, and I provide evidence to support that in my book *Reincarnation: The Missing Link in Christianity.*[2] So if you want to know exactly what the Church fathers did with reincarnation, you can read that book. Many Jews of Jesus' day believed in reincarnation. If Jesus had rejected the idea, he would have explained why. Yet there is no record of Jesus denying reincarnation in scripture. Instead, there are several places where he teaches it, both in the New Testament and in other scriptures. In the second century, there were a number of Christian groups who believed in reincarnation. It wasn't until the third century that the Church began to reject the belief.

Why is reincarnation the missing link in Christianity? Everywhere you turn, you are making decisions, you are loving or not loving, you are hating or not hating, you will forgive or not forgive, you will help someone or not help someone. Earth is a schoolroom, and recording angels are noting all of our actions. But sometimes it takes ten thousand years for karma to return to us because things come back often in very wide orbits. Or it could come back an hour from now. Without karma and reincarnation, life doesn't make sense to us. You wonder, "What did I ever do to deserve these terrible circumstances?" Or even, "What did I do to earn this incredible windfall?"

....

"What has become of Henry Ford? He is not in embodiment at this time [1992]. He is studying in the higher levels of learning in the universities of the spirit on the etheric plane. And no doubt he is studying exactly what he needs to be studying to finally deal with the ability to be loving and the ability to be ruthless. And he will no doubt reincarnate again to complete his mission."[3]   Elizabeth Clare Prophet

....

Multiple Opportunities

This brings us to another reason why reincarnation is important: You have a divine potential. Your destiny is to become one with God. Almost every belief system that teaches reincarnation also teaches that man has the potential for union with God. This divine potential is described as a seed or spark within us that needs to be nurtured or fanned so that it can develop into full Godhood.

Mystics have described a process of returning to the state

of primordial bliss that we knew before we ever made the choice to be separate from God. Every time you have a feeling of oneness with all of life, you have come closer to the goal of oneness with God. I will share more about how to achieve this oneness later on.

The reason that we need reincarnation is that most people's lives are cut short before they reach the goal of this mystical union. Reincarnation also provides opportunity for people who do not want to seek God in a particular life. Maybe they're not ready. Maybe they had a bad experience in childhood or in a past life. Reincarnation provides us chance after chance to learn our lessons and make further spiritual progress with each successive incarnation. Our trials in life—whether they concern our health, our finances, our profession, or our loved ones—give us the needed opportunities for developing self-mastery.

Let's explore the ramifications of reincarnation and what difference it can make in our ideas about our life today. Reincarnation needs to be a working part of our philosophy. It is part of a belief system that helps answer many of the questions that we may be asking ourselves: Why am I here? Why do I have the parents that I do? Why am I afraid of airplanes? Why do I like banana splits? What do I want to do with my life?

The Pre-Life Review

The soul's pre-life review before once more descending into a physical body is a preparation for what she must accomplish. This preparation is indelibly impressed upon our soul and our memory body (which, if you remember, is our etheric body, the highest vibrating of our four lower bodies) so that when we meet people and come into situations, we sense we have a responsibility to them. This is why we may walk the last mile with people even while all of our friends say, "Well, why do you put up with that person and why do you get involved in these kinds of situations where everybody is using you?" and that sort of thing. The soul knows where her karmic debts are and what she has to do in order to be liberated from a particular tie to someone or some situation. Not that the tie (such as marriage) must necessarily be broken at the end of that responsibility, but there is a new kind of bonding, a bonding of freedom instead of bondage to the karmic circumstance.

During your pre-life review, you are given one or more options for a life plan that will bring you into contact with those you have wronged, and that will give you opportunities to accomplish the divine plan for your life. We don't get away with the wrongs, the hatreds, the things that we are really fed up with or that make us tense. They follow us. We reincarnate, and we must deal with our wrongs again.

Imagine that you have just come forth from your mother's womb, and the mother living next door to you brings forth her child. Lo and behold, here you are with the very person you may have been fighting with in your last life. You may have an immediate dislike for one another. It has started all over again, giving you another opportunity to make peace with one another. So there really is no escape. We must make our peace with God and man. This is the only way out of the karmic knot.

....

As long as a person is unsuccessful
in his purpose in this world,
the Holy One, blessed be He, uproots him
and replants him over and over again.

ZOHAR I

....

The more karma you have balanced, the more freedom you will have to accomplish your divine plan. In the East, this plan is known as your *dharma,* your sacred work or duty. The way to stop reincarnating so that you can remain in the beautiful heaven-world is to balance your karma and fulfill your dharma. Your dharma may be to work as a healer and to make new discoveries in healing. Or it may require you to bring a number of children into the world. Or you may be an artist, a sculptor, an engineer, a teacher. Once you get on the spiritual path and begin to balance your karma, your Higher Self will help you to figure out your dharma.

Let me note that it's getting more and more difficult for people to serve each other in karmic situations according to their pre-life review and the choices that they have made. This is because there are so many abortions. People who plan to reincarnate at the same time to resolve karmic debts with one another are not able to do so. This can seriously delay the time-table for certain karma to be balanced.

Opportunity Lost

Because many of us have been told that Jesus is the only one who has God in him and that we can only achieve salvation *through* him, not by becoming *like* him, there is a prevailing sense of the worthlessness of life. It is very subtle and it is subconscious.

If people knew that they really are God walking around—that God is their mind and their heart and their spirit and that their bodies are the bodies of the Divine Mother—they would have a sense of sacredness about their life and their being and a sense of sacredness about their offspring. They would know that a physical body is not just to be done away with in suicide or in abortion but that the body is the temple of the living God.

The soul requires that envelope of the physical body to go through its evolution upon earth.

When we abort a life in the womb, we are aborting the opportunity of a soul whose timetable has come to be on earth at that precise moment. Many children come into life assigned to adoptive parents in accordance with their pre-life review. They may not even be intended to live with their biological parents. So we need to make it comfortable for women to have their babies, for them to go back to their natural sensitivity to life. I've seen souls leave the body after abortion. They are traumatized, they are crying, and not just because of the pain but because they so needed to be born and to be in life at that particular time.

Being a co-creator with God is a tremendous responsibility. As we become insensitive to the unborn we become insensitive to euthanasia, to suicide, to all of these other means of terminating life, instead of allowing the timing to be God's prerogative. God, through the Holy Spirit, gives the breath of life and takes away the breath of life. I am not against family planning or against birth control measures. But abortion is not a birth control measure.

We are just like that life in the womb. We are helpless babes. We are given the womb of this cosmos to survive in. We are just as helpless as tiny babes before nuclear war or dread diseases or cancer. And we may also be taken abruptly from our physical life. The point I am making is that not one of us has permanent identity in God until we attain to that reunion with God. This is the opportunity that the child in the womb is seeking, and this is what we are seeking. So as we are merciless toward others who need their life, we will see that karma return to us. And today, I am afraid, we see that karma returning to our nation and to all of the nations of the world.

I have no condemnation whatsoever in saying this. I understand how many people have been caught up in the notion of a woman's right to privacy and abortion. But I ask you to reconsider this as you think about the near-death experiences that I have described and how precious life is to God for him to have given people these experiences. Let us all recognize that the preciousness of life is the same—whether for a child in the womb or for any of us.

A Calculated Risk

And with me They [then] made a compact;
In my heart wrote it, not to forget it:
If you go down into Egypt,
And thence you bring the one Pearl—
The Pearl that lies in the Sea,
Hard by the loud-breathing Serpent—
Then shalt Thou put on thy Robe
And thy Mantle that goeth upon it,
And with thy Brother, Our Second,
Shall thou be Heir in our Kingdom.

"THE HYMN OF THE PEARL," JUDAS THOMAS THE APOSTLE

The soul reincarnating, coming back into this physical level because of the karma that must be balanced, is a calculated risk. You take the calculated risk. You take it because you must. Your soul is that pearl in the "The Hymn of the Pearl," one of the greatest of all Gnostic writings.[4] The pearl is lost in the sea of the astral plane. You must go down and find that pearl and rescue it. It's the pearl of great price. What is its price? This is a world where things appear one way one day and another way the next.

Nothing is clear. Everything is in motion. It's like being under the sea, where the size and shape of the fish and the sea life is distorted. We cannot see clearly.

Before incarnation, when you're in the octaves of light and full of fervor, you are determined to go down and do it this time—to raise up your soul, to integrate with it, to draw this soul to the level of your Higher Self, to balance your karma. Then you enter your next incarnation and begin life on earth once more, and you get into the records of old karma and old desires and especially old resentments and old hurts and anger against this one and that one because they did you wrong in a past life.

Suddenly all of this turmoil is going into your feeling world. You begin to feel this entrenched sense: "I don't want anybody telling me what to do. I don't want to be under that person. I don't want to be born to these parents. I don't want to have to marry this person. I don't want to have to give birth to this person." These feelings happen because you are experiencing the recorded memories of your emotional body.

At the moment of birth a veil of forgetfulness descends upon you because God wants you to have a clean white page to write on so that you only need to deal with this life. Most people would not be capable of dealing with conscious memories of intense traumas and tragedies from their past lives. But in one sense you cannot avoid encountering them because in this life you are still the sum of all that you have ever been in those lives. So at the level of the subconscious or unconscious psyche, you have nonresolution and fears, and these may rise to overtake you, causing emotional upsets, neuroses, and phobias.

A Classic Love Triangle through the Centuries

I would like to tell you a fictional story, a kind of parable about karma and reincarnation. This story illustrates why it is important for us to understand reincarnation and what it can tell us about life after death. It's the story of three souls—Jeanne, Simon, and Percival—in a classic love triangle. The setting is late twelfth-century France near the town of Ypres (in present-day Belgium).

The Beginning of a Chain of Lives

Simon is a noble. Percival is the landless, second son of a lesser noble, a vassal of Simon, and Jeanne is the daughter of a friend of Simon. Jeanne spends much time at the court of the Count of Flanders, a place of music, feasts, and nonstop entertainment. She enjoys meat-stuffed pastries and delicacies of spun sugar. Her father betroths her to Simon, a knight ten years older than she is, whose barren wife has just died.

Meanwhile, Jeanne falls in love with Percival without telling him that she is betrothed to his liege lord. Simon catches them together and beats Percival severely. Jeanne is forced to marry Simon immediately. He takes her away to live at his fortresslike château and tells her that she cannot leave the château until she bears him an heir. She is angry at being kept from the happy court life she had come to enjoy.

Things settle down for a few years. Then it becomes obvious that Jeanne is not producing an heir. Simon begins to reject her and to beat her for her barrenness. He is also cruel to their servants. He enjoys forcing them to lie on the ground while he stands on their backs, kicks them with his spurs, and orders them to bark like dogs.

In despair, Jeanne appeals to Percival to help her escape, but Percival has married and become one of Simon's vassals. In exchange for a small parcel of land, Percival must pay taxes to Simon and fight in his wars. Percival and his placid, capable wife have several children, and he spends all of his time farming his small estate, which has few serfs. He is too timid to help Jeanne and does not want to upset the status quo, even though he loves her.

Jeanne begins to lose her will to live. She spends much of her time in prayer, both in church and at the *prie-dieu*[5] in her chambers. One day she decides that she will eat nothing but the Eucharist, a common practice among medieval women.

Although some saints are recorded as having fasted and survived for great lengths of time on only the Eucharist, Jeanne is not a saint. Her decision to fast rose out of her anger and depression rather than her spirituality. As she becomes weaker through fasting, she begins to look forward to death, even to welcome it. She believes that after death she will be with Jesus and the saints in heaven. She imagines it as a kind of heavenly court where she could feast and enjoy herself every day.

Eventually, Jeanne dies. We need to underscore the fact that her death is really a suicide. As I told you earlier, if someone dies by suicide, God may send that one immediately back into embodiment and require them to pick up where they left off. But now the individual's karma is heavier because the karma of having taken one's own life must be balanced.

Simon is happy because he is free to marry again and hopefully beget an heir. Percival is overwhelmed with feelings of remorse and powerlessness that there was nothing he could do to prevent Jeanne's death.

After death, Jeanne's soul does see Jesus. She is comforted and loved by him and spends some time in heavenly gardens with angels. But by and by she is told that she must again return to earth.

What we see here is that we return to earth because we have not completed our cycles, because we have made negative karma and we must balance that karma with positive karma. Thinking that going to Jesus is the solution to all of our problems, whether through suicide or self-starvation, is simply not going to work. Let no hour, no moment of temptation, bring you to the brink of self-destruction, because right around the corner is the joy of salvation, whether through Jesus Christ, Gautama Buddha, or Lord Maitreya.

So, back to the story, Jeanne is reborn in 1340. When she is just eight years old, the plague strikes France. She must watch as her parents, brothers, sisters, and grandmother die. She runs away in fear and finally dies of cold and starvation.

What went wrong with Jeanne? If she had had an understanding of karma and reincarnation, she might not have given up on life only to be reborn into worse suffering than before. That's what can happen to those who try to escape life's lessons, especially through suicide.

We need never give up our physical bodies, no matter how horrible our lives may be. All of us have had hardships and deep pain. None of us have truly escaped this unless we have very, very good karma. So life is here to teach us many lessons, and we need to embrace those lessons even if they are hard and painful. Rather than step aside from them, we can walk straight to them, challenge them, gain resolution, and move on.

It is only while we are living that we can use our free will to make significant spiritual progress. However nice it may be on the other side, it is only a place of rest and preparation, not of change and resolution.

If Jeanne had understood karma, she might have decided to see her life as a learning experience rather than collapsing in despair. Again, suicide truly is the ultimate selfishness. It takes courage to admit that you have created your own destiny, but this is just what we must do if we want to evolve spiritually.

Another Chance

The wonderful thing about reincarnation is that it gives us yet another chance to tackle our problems, and it gives the same chance to the three characters in our story. These characters are born with their problems relatively intact. Jeanne, Simon, and Percival reenter the stage of life in 1895 in Windsor, southern Ontario, Canada. Their names are Jean, Simon, and Perry.

In school, Jean has a crush on Perry, but he's always too shy to speak to her. Simon sees Jean and develops a strong urge to possess and dominate her. Simon is strong, athletic, and popular. Perry is shy and reserved. Jean has a strange attraction/repulsion to Simon, but she feels a stronger tie to Perry. She rejects Simon and begins to date Perry.

Jean and Perry's romance is halted by World War I. In 1914 Perry heads off to war, as does Simon, both serving in Canada's First Division. Simon taunts Perry about his courage, just as he has done since grade school. Perry secretly wonders whether he will be able to fight.

They are on the front lines during the second battle of Ypres when the Germans first use poison gas. As the French are enveloped by the cloud that slowly creeps along the ground, the soldiers scatter, gasping and vomiting. Many of the Canadians are asphyxiated. Some on the fringes survive by wrapping their heads in handkerchiefs and burying their faces in the ground.

Some of the men decide to fight. They wrap their heads in

wet cloths and charge into the cloud of gas. At the last minute, Perry follows them. Most of them are overcome by the gas. Perry nearly collapses but makes it back to the Canadian lines. A wide gap has opened in the lines and the Germans are pouring through. Perry rallies a group of soldiers, including Simon, to fight the Germans. They save the day by holding the gap until reinforcements can be rushed in, but Perry has breathed too much gas and dies a few days later. Perry's show of bravery, however, is a turning point for him.

Simon goes home to Canada and marries Jean. They emigrate to Detroit, where he eventually starts a small shoe factory. Jean settles in as a housewife. After a few years, it becomes apparent that once again she cannot have children. Simon has also not changed much since medieval France in terms of his brutality. Jean realizes Simon's brutal nature but can't figure out how to escape from him. She retreats into alcohol, and eventually she kills them both by driving their car into a tree on their way home from a party.

After Perry's death in a muddy trench in Belgium, he is in shock. He doesn't experience a tunnel or a life review. Instead, his soul sleeps for a long time. This happens to many people who have sudden accidents or severe situations in their transition from the physical body. Some souls are just not ready to accept the fact of their death, or they may be too lost in illusion to believe that life continues. These souls go through a period of sleep or healing before their life review.

At the end of each of your hundreds of lives, you may have said to yourself some variant of the question, "I'm dead. Now what?" But it also may have been some time after your death before you were able to consciously ask the question.

When Perry's soul wakes up, he finds himself in a room that

glows a pinkish white. He feels warm, surrounded by a fluffy comforter that looks like blue cotton candy. He slowly opens his eyes and sits up, wondering where he is. He looks down at his body. In shape, it is like the body he wore on earth, but it is nearly transparent. He discovers that he is naked, but as soon as he thinks to himself that he should have some clothes on, he is neatly dressed in his army uniform.

A man in battle fatigues appears to Perry and begins to speak. "Congratulations, son! You did a good job."

"I did?" says Perry, somewhat bewildered.

"Sure! You saved many men from being killed. If you hadn't held that gap in the line, the war would have been much worse. It was touch and go. We weren't sure you had it in you. You're going to find that your next life will be much better because you were able to summon up your courage."

"My next life?" Perry asks, confused.

"That's right," says the man. "Your next life."

"Is this heaven, then?" asks Perry.

"You could call it that," answers the man. "But you can't stay here forever."

"Then who are you?" asks Perry.

"I'm your guiding spirit, an angel, if you like."

"You don't look like an angel," Perry says.

The man begins to glow. His fatigues disappear and are replaced by a white robe. "Is this better?" he asks.

"Yes. May I ask your name?" says Perry.

"You can call me Francis," says the angel. "I didn't want to frighten you by showing you this form before you realized that you were dead."

"What year is it?" Perry asks.

"It's 1924, by your reckoning," says Francis.

Perry slowly realizes that he has been asleep for nine years. Francis takes Perry to a small but elegant blue and white hall in a large, university-type complex. Here Perry first reviews all of the actions of his past life. Perry asks to see Jean and the scene switches to Jean and Simon's home. They are not fighting, but Perry can sense the overwhelming depression that has invaded Jean's soul. He is saddened. Francis tells him not to worry, that he will have a chance to see her soon.

In the meantime, Perry gets the opportunity to work on developing his courage. Francis takes him to a place where he can imagine and create different scenarios in which to overcome his fear. First he imagines himself as a Hercules-type giant, ten feet tall, who goes around the country protecting the weak. He modifies the scene of his beating by Simon, repeating it over and over until he is able to prevail as his own self. He finds that he is no longer afraid of Simon.

One day, Francis appears and tells Perry that this phase of his training is over and that he can now meet the soul of Jean. It is 1932, and Simon and Jean have just died in the car wreck.

Simon is angry. His first thought is, "That stupid bitch!" He finds himself in a twisted version of his life in Michigan where he is somehow all-powerful. He makes it more bizarre. He populates it with slaves who attend to his every whim. Simon has found himself at level six of the astral plane.

One day, an angel wearing men's clothing walks into Simon's office. "Come with me so that you can learn and grow," the angel says. Simon tells two of his henchmen to throw the angel out the window. Simon sits at his desk, smoking cigars and making deals until his world begins to fade. Then he wakes up as a screaming baby. The year is 1958.

At first, Jean doesn't realize that she is dead. She finds herself in a land very much like suburban Michigan. Then as she wanders down the street, she sees a medieval knight riding towards her. She looks up and sees that it's Perry. She swings up onto the back of his horse and they gallop off together, suddenly finding themselves in a world that is like a tourist postcard version of medieval France. It is clean, sparkling, and free of disease.

Perry fights in a tournament and wins Jean's hand. Then she and Perry live in a castle and have many children. She is happy for a time, but she doesn't seem to be able to sleep at night. She has nightmares of crashing into something, but she doesn't remember what a car is.

One morning Jean wakes up sobbing, and suddenly her world begins to dissolve like a watercolor in the rain. She doesn't know where Perry is. She finds herself on an endless, barren plain. She walks for what seems like days. Finally, she sees an oasis. She goes toward it, and there is a man (the same angel who appeared to Perry) in a monk's robe sitting at the edge of a well. Suddenly she realizes that she is thirsty. She can't remember the last time she drank anything.

"May I have a drink, please?" she says.

"You may only drink if you are ready to wake up," he replies.

"I am awake, aren't I?" she says.

"You are asleep," he says. "You have been asleep for many lifetimes. Do you want to wake up?"

She thinks about it. "Can I go back to Perry and my children and the castle?" she asks.

"Yes," he says. "But it won't be real. And you will know that it's not real. Perry wasn't like that in that life. He was too timid to have you."

"If I wake up, will I see Perry?"

"There are no guarantees," the man replies. "The only thing

I can promise you is that you will never be with the real Perry unless you do wake up."

She takes a deep breath, dips water out of a bucket from the well, and drinks a long drink. Suddenly the landscape changes. What was once gray and barren is now teeming with life. She is in a beautiful garden in late autumn, filled with the scent of ripening fruit. The man changes too, beginning to glow within with an internal light.

She asks him many questions. "Why have I never been able to have children?"

"You have had children. But the last three lifetimes have been childless. The causes are connected to your previous lifetimes."

He waves his hand, and a screen seems to materialize out of the air and float over the grass. On the screen appear scenes from her past. Carefully he shows her the cause of her sorrows—her own neglect of her family in a previous life and her abandonment of Perry.

"Will I ever be able to make it right?" she asks.

"That is up to you," he says. Francis tells her that she must pursue spiritual development and oneness with God. "That is the only way to overcome the barriers that exist between you and Perry," he says.

"Show me how," she begs.

"I can teach you many things here, but you will have to find a teacher to remind you of it while you are on earth."

Soon Jean is allowed to see Perry. Now they have their reunion, and it is a joyful one. But it is tainted by their knowledge that it will not last. Francis asks Jean and Perry to come with him to one of the classrooms at a spiritual learning center in the heaven-world. They review the strengths and weaknesses in their characters and plan how they will overcome them in their next life.

Francis tells them that it will not be easy. "You will find that you will be blinded to your true nature at first. You will only be able to find love together if you discover it inside of yourselves."

He gives them a glimpse of other worlds that they can journey to in their future lives, and he shows them how their love can eventually help to sustain and inspire an entire city. They vow to each other to balance their karma together in their next life so that they can move on to this happier future.

Francis takes them to a green and purple room called the embarkation area, a room with many doorways. He sends Perry through one door and Jean through another. They feel themselves walking into a tunnel of light. They begin to feel themselves being elongated and sucked downwards. Before long, they feel the unrelenting pressure of the birth canal, and they begin to forget their experiences in the afterlife.

Seeing Each Other as Spiritual Beings

Simon is reborn into a large family where no one notices him. This is torture for him, of course, because he wants to be noticed. He becomes very flamboyant and ends up as a used-car dealer who sells drugs on the side. But he's always dreaming of that one great deal that will make him rich. Thus he's never happy with his lot. He crosses paths with Jean and asks her out, but she won't even speak to him.

Jean is born in Detroit and brought up in a liberal Protestant household. Her family goes to church at Christmas and Easter, and that's about it. She is pretty, popular, and enjoys parties and fun, but she develops an eating disorder in her teens. By her late teens her eating disorder has grown into full-on bulimia.

She compulsively stuffs herself with doughnuts, pastries, and fast food, only to vomit it back up.

Jean's eating disorder arises not so much out of fear of being fat as it does out of guilt about enjoying food. Nevertheless, she makes it through college and law school, dating many men but never sticking with anyone for very long. She doesn't want them to find out about her disease.

Perry is now gifted with a strong drive in this life. He's good at sports, handsome, and well-liked in high school. He becomes a successful attorney, dates many women, but doesn't find the "right" one. Jean comes to work at his firm. He is immediately attracted to her but unaccountably afraid. They begin dating and fall in love.

At first, everything seems wonderful. They are pleasantly surprised to find that they both like brie and medieval French poetry. But then he finds that his sense of unease is growing. He needs to have a drink or two in order to feel relaxed around Jean. Soon he can't even make love to her without a couple of drinks. Then he becomes impotent. It was a problem he'd had occasionally before, but now it won't go away.

Jean doesn't know what to do. She is unaccountably afraid that she will never be able to have children. She doesn't understand this fear since her mother had five children. Then Perry discovers her bulimia, and he backs off from her. They are both miserable but unable to figure out how to be together.

Jean decides that she is not cut out to be a lawyer and starts looking for other work. She goes into treatment to try to get over her bulimia. After six months in a treatment center, she seems to have gotten the physical part of the problem under control. She forces herself to eat regular meals and to keep them down. But she still has baffling fears about eating and enjoying herself.

Trying to get to the bottom of her problems, Jean begins working with a psychologist. She can't remember anything in her current life that could have led to her current problems. Her childhood was untraumatic, almost boring in its regularity.

Jean begins reading a variety of self-help books. Then she learns about the science of the spoken Word and the violet flame. She begins using the mantra, "I AM a being of violet fire, I AM the purity God desires!" every day. Gradually she finds more time to add other decrees. Jean enjoys the feeling of lightness that the violet flame brings, and she notices that her life seems to be changing. She remembers when she first lost her will to live. Slowly, she loses some of her fear. Although she doesn't consciously remember her entire medieval lifetime, she remembers that Perry was afraid to love her.

Radiant Spiral Violet Flame

In the name of Almighty God and my own Higher Self, I call for the violet flame to blaze through my whole being and world to dissolve all that is less than God's perfect plan for me: [insert your personal prayers here]

> *Radiant spiral violet flame*
> *Descend, now blaze through me!*
> *Radiant spiral violet flame,*
> *Set free, set free, set free!*

> *Radiant violet flame, O come,*
> *Expand and blaze thy light through me!*
> *Radiant violet flame, O come,*
> *Reveal God's power for all to see!*
> *Radiant violet flame, O come,*
> *Awake the earth and set it free!*

Radiance of the violet flame,
  Expand and blaze through me!
Radiance of the violet flame,
  Expand for all to see!
Radiance of the violet flame,
  Establish mercy's outpost here!
Radiance of the violet flame,
  Come, transmute now all fear!

In full faith I thankfully accept this manifest right here and now with full power, eternally sustained, and all-powerfully active!

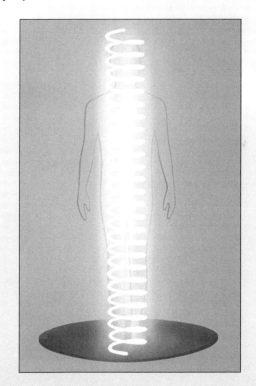

Meanwhile, Perry goes through a period of soul-searching. He doesn't date anyone after Jean. He starts meditating and begins to feel more at peace. He reaches a point of calm strength and feels that he is without fear.

Three years after they first broke up, Perry calls Jean out of the blue. They talk and share their experiences with each other. She tells him about decrees, he tells her about meditation, and they begin to use them together. Finally, they decide to give their relationship another try, and they start to see each other as spiritual beings.

You know, it's a wonderful thing when you can see another person as a spiritual being. You find a whole new dimension about that person, things that don't necessarily come out when we're operating at the strictly human level.

At last, Jean becomes pregnant. She carries the baby to term with few problems. But as the baby is being born in the hospital, Jean starts to hemorrhage. She loses consciousness, and the doctors think that she is dying.

She feels herself being sucked through a dark tunnel toward a bright light. She sees a being of light, and suddenly it all comes back to her. She remembers her life plan and the vow she made with Perry. She realizes that the being in the light is Francis, who spoke to her at the well. She feels an incredible sense of peace, but she fights it.

"Didn't I do it right this time, Francis? I got over my fear of living, didn't I? I worked on my relationship to God, and you were right—it did bring Perry closer to me. Why do I have to die now? I don't want to leave Perry and my baby," Jean cries.

"You don't have to die, Jean. You are being given this experience so that you will remember this feeling of love and share it with others," Francis assures her. Gratefully, Jean basks in Francis' warm radiance before gently sinking back into her body.

The Convergence of Cosmos

Imagine all the people in your life on rings of importance. Those closest to you are on the inner rings. As the rings go out, it is as though you were a great atom with many electron shells. If you regard people to be more on the periphery of your life, they are way off in the distance on the outermost ring.

Yet all of these people, groups, societies, universities, institutions—everything on earth is integral to the balancing of your karma. All those things must return to that point from which you can get into a situation where you are with your group of souls, have some association on the inner or the outer, and balance karma personally.

Think about everything that has happened to you in this lifetime alone—the people you have met, what you have seen, where you have been, the influences upon you, what has led you to be the person you are. All of this is what I call the *convergence of cosmos*. For you and you alone, the whole cosmos has converged at a point in time and space to save a single soul—your soul. You just have to know by the very fact of being in this body, being in incarnation, that this is the optimum opportunity that God could give you to come to resolution with every part of life.

It is the wisdom of God to return to us over and over again the fruits of our consciousness until we finally bend the knee to the immutable law of karma. Lifetime after lifetime we return to the physical plane of existence where we have qualified God's light, energy, and consciousness, there to experience the consequences of our actions and ultimately to decide to be only God —to live and move and have our being in him simply because we are his offspring.

The Joy of Karma

There are many, many karmic issues that one might have other than the ones in the story that I shared with you earlier. Some karma may involve wrongs that you did in a past life that you can hardly imagine you would ever have done. Or possibly even in this life you may have changed for reasons that you know, but you still have guilt that you can't seem to get over.

You may die a thousand deaths, so to speak, over something you did that you know was wrong. But in order to atone for this, you must do more than suffer. After Saul stood by, consenting to the stoning of Saint Stephen, he lived out his lifetime as the apostle Paul, a servant of Christ and shepherd of souls. No one will question his good works as an apostle. But for his consenting to the death of Stephen (in addition to the karma of previous lives), he had to reincarnate as Saint Hilarion and become a healer. As Hilarion, he needed to heal again and again, performing miracles and exorcisms for thousands, before the law of karma was satisfied and he could receive his final reward in his soul's ascension to the heart of God.[6]

But Paul enjoyed his lifetime as Hilarion. That's the thing about balancing karma—it's a joyous path because you have the sense that you are paying your bills, fully and finally, and for the last time. It's how you feel when you can pay all your bills at the end of the month, only better. When you go through life giving to others, you do it for the sake of loving. You don't think about it as karma, but your soul knows and expresses profound joy to be paying her debts in dignity. You are being responsible, you are being accountable, you are alleviating pain and serving to set life free. This brings you to the great discovery of the mystery of the kingdom of God within you.

You can establish a certain joyful mind-set about settling your karma to reach the best possible place in your afterlife and give the following prayer fervently:

> *Whatever it takes, my beloved mighty I AM Presence, Almighty God, I am going to get to the etheric octave, and I demand that I be given the opportunity to transmute my karma that would hold me and bind me to the astral plane, even to the first level of the astral plane. And I ask you to show me what I must do to pay all my debts to anyone, anywhere who is in the astral plane, whether in physical incarnation or in any of those levels.*

If you resolve your karma made with people who live in the astral plane and are of it, then, you see, you don't have the ties and the obligations to enter that plane in order to pay your debts. It is much preferable to pay those debts while in physical incarnation, because when you are out of physical incarnation it is much easier to get lost in the astral plane while you are attempting to balance karma there.

Forgiveness

Although we cannot go back twenty or sixty years or to another lifetime and undo what we have done, what we can do is call forth the violet flame—that spiritual energy, the fire of the Holy Spirit that is for transmutation. The records of these pains and hurts can be consumed in our own four lower bodies, our own records, the subconscious, the psyche, and also in the life of anyone who may have been emotionally or otherwise injured according to how we have acted. We can send that violet flame to anyone who has ever been burdened by something we have done. And that violet flame will be a gift from our hearts and

God's heart to give that one permanent healing. I know that is the profound desire of all of us.

Forgiveness is the nature of the violet flame. You can't give violet flame for someone who has wronged you and expect change if you harbor at some level of your being negative feelings about that person.

You may have forgiven someone on the conscious level, but the subconscious and the unconscious lag behind. Old resentments, angers, hurts, and a sense of injustice are still there. So the rational, thinking part of our being says, "OK, I forgive you. You rammed your car into my child and he was killed. I understand that you couldn't have prevented the accident. I forgive you." But you don't forgive because some part of your being is in such pain over the loss of your child. You may even unconsciously direct your anger against God for allowing it to happen.

We see this in many people's lives over various traumatic experiences. A woman who has everything in life—a wonderful husband, money, society—suddenly loses her husband to cancer and she's left alone. Although she doesn't verbalize it, and she may not even be aware of it, she has changed and never utters the name of God again. What is really going on at the unconscious level is a momentum of anger—against whom? Against God. This filters through in moods, temperaments, and reactions to other people. And it never reaches resolution.

Until we can say to Almighty God, "I am profoundly hurt. Why do I have this illness? Why did I lose my home? I don't understand why you let this happen to me. Nevertheless, I will say, 'true and righteous are thy judgments.'" The acceptance of the will of God is absolutely necessary. If you are not resolved with God, then you really are not resolved with the God who resides within you or within your fellow man. We may pay lip service to forgiveness, but until the whole psyche is healed and the karma is balanced, there is not total resolution.

Not Everything Is Bad Karma

We never really know who was the innocent victim or the victimizer from a previous life. Life is intricate, and not everything can be categorized into neat generalities. Yes, we need to be accountable, even for actions in past lives that we do not remember. But there are other possible causes of karmic ties. People initiate new acts of negative karma every day. The key is in our reactions to these things that test our spiritual mettle. They allow us to see if we have truly mastered our emotions and our ego, our old hurts and psychological triggers. God doesn't do anything without a profound purpose. Accepting that can help us to avoid the sense of injustice that can only make matters worse.

We also may find that someone is jealous of our loving relationships, creative projects, or achievements. An important part of the spiritual path is learning to deal with this sometimes very subtle challenge in our lives. In other cases, we may need to experience certain things in order to get in touch with the pain that others bear, so we can rise to a new level of understanding and compassion. Or it may be a sacrifice so that someone else can learn and grow. In other words, we can never point an accusing finger. We can't assume that someone who is healthy is a saint or that someone who is sick is a sinner. We can never assume that someone who is rich has good karma and another person who is poor has bad karma. Our perspective is not always the perspective of the soul.

What we have to do is to pursue mercy and justice and equal treatment for all people. We need to help those who are bowed down, those who mourn, those whose psychology is messed up because they have been both victim and victimizer. We all have the crisscrossing of scars on our psyche that we have to contend with as we lead our daily lives. We have to invoke the violet flame for universal, world, and personal transmutation of the records of karma as we serve to set life free. And when we send forth violet flame and forgiveness, it resides in our own worlds and acts as a buffer against negative karma or harm.

Seeing Your Past Lives in the Cosmic Mirror

You read examples of incarnations in the story I told you earlier, and now you know about the violet flame. But what about resolving the karma of your own past lives? This will take some work on your psychology. Only when you have sufficiently prepared yourself spiritually for a psychological probe of past circumstances affecting current events in your life will an ascended master lead you before the cosmic mirror in one of their retreats when you leave the body at night.

I'll give you a bit of an idea about what happens when you are ready for this experience: A portion of a past life, or more than one, passes before you. Instantly you are aware of the ramifications of your karma even as you relive the emotions, the premeditated thoughts, and the acts themselves. It could be a painful experience, but your Higher Self stands gently but firmly supporting you to face the future with a hope based on the scientific knowledge that in your hands, by the grace of the Holy Spirit, lies the power to change.

You soon see the need to apply the violet flame to those scenes and memories until balance is restored. And you know that you have work to do. The master tells you to go back to your physical body, where the physical karma was made, and work things out by divine love and the violet flame. When the necessary clearance of the emotional and mental bodies is accomplished, the master says you will be ready for the next session of therapy.

One ascended master who gives his students this kind of experience in his etheric retreat promises, "The lessons learned by the soul out of the body during sleep are not lost but become a part of the composite of subconscious self-awareness, surfacing just enough to prick the soul memory and prod it to decisive action."[7]

The quickening of the outer mind to this inner soul experience, once it has returned to waking consciousness and the five senses, is accomplished by the master through the associative technique, or the arrangement of uncanny circumstances that turn loose the soul memory, sometimes in a torrent of emotions, as major turning points in her evolution and karma are relived and then relieved through the violet flame.

....

Who Is Saint Germain?

Saint Germain is a master alchemist and teacher of masters and men. He is also known in the heaven-world as a diplomat, expressing the godly qualities of dignity, grace, gentility, poise, and true statesmanship. His name comes from the Latin *Sanctus Germanus,* meaning simply "Holy Brother." As chohan, or lord, of the seventh ray, the violet ray, Saint Germain initiates our souls in the science and ritual of transmutation through the violet flame.

Saint Germain says: "I am an ascended being, but it has not ever been thus. Not once or twice but for many incarnations I walked the earth as you now do, confined to mortal frame and the limitations of dimensional existence. I was on Lemuria and I was on Atlantis. I have seen civilizations rise and fall. I have seen the undulations of consciousness as mankind have cycled from golden ages to primitive societies. I have seen the choices, and I have seen mankind by wrong choices squander the energies of a hundred thousand years of scientific advancement and even degrees of cosmic consciousness that transcend that which is attained by members of the most advanced religions of the day.

"Yes, I have seen the choices, and I have chosen. By right choices man and woman establish their position in hierarchy. By choosing to be free in the magnificent will of God, I won my freedom from that mortal round of incarnations and justifications of an existence outside the One. I won my freedom by that flame, that keynote of the Aquarian cycle traced by alchemists of old, that purple elixir the saints do hold.

"You are mortal. I am immortal. The only difference between us is that I have chosen to be free, and you have yet to make the choice. We have the same potential, the same resources, the same connection to the One. I have taken mine to forge a God-identity." [8]

Once again you stand before the cosmic mirror as Saint Germain shows you the original blueprint of your divine plan, the plan that was imprinted upon your etheric body when you were conceived in the heart of God. And so you learn another reason for reviewing your past lives one by one: to determine what portion of that divine plan you have brought forth thus far and what portion you have not.

Saint Germain tells you, "You can call forth the talents you have developed in past ages, for these are stored as treasure [in heaven]...." He assures you that bringing forth these talents does not depend upon your recalling through your outer memory. But he also cautions you that your use of these spiritual resources is subject to the law of karma once they are made available to you. [9]

CHAPTER 8

Integrating It All

The disciples said to Jesus: Tell us how our end will be.
Jesus said: Have you then discovered the beginning,
so that you inquire about the end?
For where the beginning is, there shall be the end.
Blessed is he who shall stand at the beginning,
and he shall know the end
and he shall not taste death.
Blessed is he who was before he came into being.

THE GOSPEL OF THOMAS, A GNOSTIC TEXT

We can all agree by now, I hope, that we are not just our physical bodies. And I hope we can challenge the notion that comes forth from Christian clergy that at the moment of conception our soul is created, which is the prevailing belief in Christianity today. Now I want to integrate the concepts that I have discussed concerning life, death, and the afterlife with who you really are and a deeper perspective.

The creation of your body was not the creation of your soul. God isn't waiting around for the moment of conception to—quick, hurry up and get out his dough—form another soul and pop it into the womb so that it will be there when that body comes out.

You are consciousness. And that consciousness passes through the cycles of the Great Causal Body, the upper figure in the Chart of Your Divine Self (see page 176), and gathers more and more of Being unto itself in the spiritual octaves. You experience the spiritual octaves first. You put on skeins of consciousness. You gather more of your God Self, your identity, your individualization of the God flame. This is how creation comes from the spiritual octaves.

And so your consciousness is born long before your soul ever inhabits these four lower bodies, this physical form. This consciousness is what people normally call their mind, but it pre-exists birth and continues to exist after death, abiding in etheric octaves between incarnations.

Why Are We Here?

What does it mean to be in physical embodiment, to be in a physical body on earth? It means that we have free will and that we can create. We can be co-creators with God and with one another. We can fulfill our desires. We can balance karma, both negative and positive. We can work change together for effective community action by using the laws of spiritual alchemy and physical chemistry and physics, and by the Holy Spirit.

To be in a physical body when our course is not yet through in this world is the most desirable state to be in. Some people who are in what has been called the New Age think that it doesn't matter whether we are in physical incarnation or not. I want to disabuse all of us of this misconception because, believe me, it does matter.

Some Christians have said to me, "Why do you worry about death? Why do you worry about what's happening in the coming decade or about nuclear war? When we die, we're all going to heaven with Jesus. Jesus is coming in his Second Coming. There's going to be a final Armageddon, perhaps a total war. And that is going to be the beginning of our true bliss." Well, the fact of the matter is that a nuclear war is not the entrance to spiritual glory and realms of light, nor is it the cessation of life on earth. Nor is it the promise of the Second Coming and not having to incarnate again.

While we are here, we are intended to create—for the good of our own souls, for the good of our communities, our families, our nations, our planet. When the sun rises each day, we can already have clear intentions for what we will do of constructive purpose for the benefit of individuals and humanity as a whole.

One reason people espouse worthy causes is that their actions are literally setting in motion causes that will have effects, in other words *karma*. Another word for *cause* is *karma*. When we set in motion good causes, good momentums, we reap the rewards of the effects that they bring to us and to all life. If we enter into these causes and projects with a spirit of service, of helping people and of doing the will of God, we will accrue a momentum of good works. Thus we can add rings to our tree of life.

The Tree of Life

What is our tree of life? It's our causal body. And by the momentum of good works that we have accrued, we increase our self-mastery and our identity.

Chart of Your Divine Self

The Chart of Your Divine Self is the Tree of Life.* At the top you can see the Great Causal Body, with its rings of light surrounding the white-fire core. These rings are actually interpenetrating spheres. The bottom figure in the Chart represents you today where you are—you in the idealized sense.

You are surrounded by the flame of the Holy Spirit, which is the violet flame. It surrounds you because you invoke it. It doesn't get there just by happenstance, because the violet flame is not native to this earth plane. It comes from God, from spiritual octaves. And so if we desire to have violet-flame blessings, we must call them forth. We can decree it, saying,

I AM a being of violet fire,
I AM the purity God desires!

Likewise, we also must call forth the cylinder of white light that you see surrounding you in this Chart in order to have it around us for protection. You can do that by using the tube of light, which I gave you earlier.

You see the crystal cord entering the top of your head in the bottom figure. The crystal cord begins in the heart of your I AM Presence at the center of your causal body and it goes all the way back to the Great Central Sun of the entire cosmos, which is called the Sun behind the sun, the spiritual sun of Being.

This tube of light looks rather like the trunk of a tree. And the light rings and rays going forth at the top look like the branches. So we can call it our tree of life. You can see that there are color rings or bands. These rings are actually spheres of light that surround your God Presence above you.

---

*To see the Chart of Your Divine Self in full color, go to https://www.summitlighthouse.org/i-am-presence/.

O people of the earth, men born and made of the elements,
but with the spirit of the Divine Man within you,
rise from your sleep of ignorance! . . .
Why have you delivered yourselves over unto death,
having power to partake of immortality? . . .
Depart from the dark light and forsake corruption forever.
Prepare yourselves to climb through the Seven Rings
and to blend your souls with the eternal Light.

HERMES TRISMEGISTUS

Our Causal Body

The Christian Bible says that "one star differeth from another star in glory."[1] Your individualized God Presence is the star that is above you in the Chart. Each one of us has a different star because these color rings, or spheres, reflect seven paths of service that we can walk to fulfill our divine plan.*

And so the blue of the outermost sphere of the causal body, which is the flame you invoke when you call to Archangel Michael, gives us the will of God. It gives us the power of God. It gives us a momentum in leadership, in anything that requires energy. And usually those who are heads of state or in the leadership in their communities or even the heads of household have a good supply in this ring of blue light.

The green of the next sphere denotes healing, science, economics, and music. It also has to do with vision, truth, and abundance in our lives.

The purple sphere combined with gold inside of the green sphere denotes the path of ministration and service, where we are ministering to life in any job or capacity from the least to the greatest, wherever we are caring for people in some way.

Closer in is the violet-flame sphere. It's the flame of the spiritual path, of the priesthood, and of churches. Violet is also the flame of spiritual alchemy and a different aspect of science as well as the color and the flame of the age of Aquarius, which has an accentuation of this flame for the next two thousand years.

The pink of the next sphere denotes every form of art, theater, drama, and music, and the expression of love in so many ways, such as compassion for one another.

Closest to the white-fire center is the yellow sphere, which shows learning, intelligence, wisdom, teachers, and those who convey knowledge in many forms.

The white ray is at the center. It is the geometry of all life, whether architecture, the building blocks of atoms, genetics— everything that has to do with the creation and its manifestation.

---

*You can refer to Appendix A to see how these seven spheres relate to the masters who teach self-mastery on the seven rays in their spiritual retreats.

What we see illustrated here in the Chart is that everything we do on earth that is positive and has a Christlike quality of dedication and selflessness—the works that we do to the glory of God and not to the glory of our own ego—the energy of these works every day will ascend to augment the spheres of our causal body.

The Importance of Physical Incarnation

At the change called death, our opportunity to qualify energy —whether adding to the treasures of our causal body or to our weight of karma—for that particular incarnation comes to an end. Then we are experiencing the results of our actions, with no ability to go back and make amends, no opportunity to say, "I'm sorry" or to say, "I love you" when we didn't tell someone, and no further opportunity to resolve our psychological problems within ourselves or with our families.

This is why physical incarnation is so important: Everything is in flux. Everything can change while you are here. You can make good. You can leave off addictions. You can call to the angels to deliver you. You can gain mastery over yourself when you set aside being self-centered and engage your Higher Self, becoming the vehicle of God's desiring on earth. In so doing you increase your identity because this causal body above you is who you really are—your Divine Self. And so, as you increase the spheres of your tree of life, you are increasing your identity and your God consciousness. You have sent your good works before you to heaven, and that becomes your heaven-world.

Almost anything we do sets something in motion that is going to have ramifications. An idle word, a careless remark, may leave someone depressed for a day or a week. We have then set up a cause. It is in motion and it is going to cycle through.

Or we may bring joy and comfort or learning or some nugget of truth to someone that gives them a burst of awareness, that raises them up. That is a different cause we may set in motion. It will ripple on and affect others. So we begin to see our ultimate accountability for what we think, feel, say, and do. Some people don't see that accountability until they have a life review after their transition.

Your Best Friend at the Life Review

As you know by now, upon the transition that is called death, we experience a life review, although this may be delayed for some souls. This review is conducted before a body of eight beings of light, brothers and sisters who have gone before us who have mastered time and space and who have been in the octaves of light for tens of thousands of years. They are magnificent God-free beings. They are called the Lords of Karma because they adjudicate how individuals deal with their karma. It is an office within the hierarchy of heaven, just as we have offices within government on earth.

....

All souls are subject to reincarnation;
and people do not know the ways
of the Holy One, blessed be He!
They do not know that they are brought
before the tribunal both before they enter
into this world and after they leave it;
they are ignorant of the many reincarnations
and secret works which they have to undergo. . . .

ZOHAR II

....

As you go before the Lords of Karma, your Holy Christ Self, which is the middle figure in the Chart, stands with you. Your Holy Christ Self is your Higher Self, the mediator between you and the absolute God-perfection of your I AM Presence in the upper figure. People who have had near-death experiences often describe a supreme being of light radiating unconditional love. As I mentioned in chapter 2, this being is most likely their own Christ Self. Your Holy Christ Self is also referred to as the Higher Mental Body, higher in the sense that it is the pure manifestation of the mind of God above you, whereas your lower mental body may be a fragmented, partial chalice for the mind of God.

The Holy Christ Self is your very best friend, your teacher. It is the still, small voice of conscience who speaks to you, warns you not to go here, not to go there, to stay away from this person, not to get involved in that relationship or that particular business deal because somehow it's not right for you or the time is not right. Even when you have no logical reason, that gut feeling that you get is a soul reading and also an inner direction from your Christ Self. When you go to sleep at night and you have a problem, and the next day or the following week suddenly all the answers come together—these are coming down from that being of light, your Holy Christ Self. So when the mind of God, individualized as each one's Holy Christ Self or Higher Mind, is functioning in the lower self, it uses the vehicle of the mental body.

So during this life review, you observe yourself and your life objectively, sustained by your Christ Self. You are shown the decisions you have made, the consequences of your actions, the good you have done and what it has brought to the world, and the negatives that you have been involved with that have been a burden to the world. This is real. And I know that your soul knows that this is real. We know it is real because we have been through it not once but many, many times because we've lived many times before.

It becomes a moment of great desiring to complete our unfinished business. Perhaps we were intended to bring forth a certain kind of cure, something through medical science, all kinds of projects that are ongoing. And our lives were cut off by an instance of karma from a previous incarnation taking us out suddenly. So we haven't been able to finish what we wanted to do.

A New Assignment

After this life review, as I explained earlier, you are assigned to a place in the heaven-world or in lower octaves that are not the heaven-world, that is commensurate with the karma of your previous life and previous incarnations. You may be assigned to a retreat of an ascended master in the etheric octaves where you can study to prepare yourself for your soul's next incarnation. This would denote having had a very high level of service and self-giving to reach those levels.

In the retreat, you would have the opportunity to balance and expand the flame in your heart, which is called the Holy Christ Flame. This is the divine spark and the very essence of our life. The expanding of our heart flame enables us to do greater good, gives us more energy, and brings us into much closer proximity and even bonding to the living Christ. In those etheric retreats, we can invoke the violet flame, we can pray, and we can gain self-mastery in the science of the spoken Word.

A certain amount of karma can be balanced out of the body when you are in the etheric retreats. But it takes a much longer time measured against earth time to balance karma when you are not in physical incarnation. The amount you can balance depends on the nature of the karma and the nature of the person. There is no set formula. So here again you can see why being in physical incarnation is so important. You are goal-fitting right now in this very moment and every day of your life, fitting yourself for where you will be at the end of this journey.

While you are in physical incarnation, as you see yourself in the lowest figure in the Chart, you are standing in direct polarity with the highest levels of the Spirit cosmos. If you are here below in the physical and your I AM Presence is at the top, the center figure in the Chart being the Presence of the living Christ, and you turn this Chart, you see that *you can bring all of God down to the physical octave, and all of you that is down here can also rise to become part of that God.* That is what it means to be in that relationship to God.

We are occupying now the lowest vibrating levels of the Matter cosmos in these dense physical bodies that we wear. But our goal is to attain reunion with the highest levels of the Spirit cosmos. So how do we get there? How can we believe that we can do this?

The Divine Ego

We must have a developed sense of self, or human ego, in order to be able to exchange it in self-confidence for the Christ mind. So self-confidence is very important. Unless you have a sense of self-worth and of the holiness of God within you—that identity that you have created, that you have built—you have nothing to exchange for the Christ-identity. You need to have created an acceptable sacrifice whereby you can receive in return, increment by increment, your individual Christhood, your Christ consciousness. It's important to know who you are and who you are not—what you are and what you are not.

The spiritual path cannot even begin until we know who we are. This is why it is so very important that parents assist their children in evolving strength of purpose—that sense that they can do things, that they can accomplish. They need to be given positive reinforcement and the disciplines necessary to truly bring out who and what they are. Children can be taught this: I am working with my mighty I AM Presence and with my Holy Christ Self, but they will not do the work for me. I must do it myself by their grace, by their love, by the gift of free will.

When you have been your own person first and have felt a sense of emptiness, of incompleteness, you realize that that human self is not really what you want. You may have graduated from college with honors. You may have been successful for many years in life. But then the day comes when you realize that this human self is limited. It can never be the infinite Self, the expanded Self. It is not a vessel for God. It must be sacrificed on the altar so that you can then receive the Real Self, the Christ Self.

This is a very important point. It is pivotal in your life, in the lives of your children, and in everyone's life. The ego is not good or bad. What we fashion the ego into may be good or bad. But the ego is a point of self-identity, the point of self-worth and self-confidence.

The Ability to Create

At every moment of the day and night we are creating. The words we put forth are our creations. They are cups carrying energy to life—the energy we qualify with our thoughts and intents, our desires and emotions, our hatred or love. All this is karma. Our actions set in motion events that have consequences and trigger other actions, which in turn have their boomerang effect.

The awareness of our mighty I AM Presence as the point of origin of God's light, energy, and consciousness going forth through our hearts, our minds, our souls, and our spirits is the beginning of our awareness of ourselves as extensions of God. I want you to be aware that your I AM Presence is above you now as the I AM THAT I AM, the focus of the eternal Source of life. And out of that Presence flows a River of Life, a moving stream of reality. It is life, energy, and consciousness. As it passes through you, you release it through your four lower bodies, through your chakras, through your words, feelings, and so forth.

And that energy goes forth. It circles the earth. It affects all life on the planet. This makes you a co-creator with God. He gave you limitless energy. He gave you free will. He gave you access to the Source and the ability to take that light and cast it in the mold of your choosing.

Only God and his offspring have the ability to create. The act of creation entails enormous responsibility. Only the law of karma will teach us just what that responsibility is. So if we want to create and are willing to take responsibility for our creations, we must accept the law of karma as the measuring rod. Our daily harvest of good and bad karma tells us the quality of our plantings.

Give Yourself a Life Review

If you want to know what I think life is all about, I will tell you. I believe that life is all about becoming a spiritual adept and dealing with those forces that challenge us and try us and attempt to move us from the seat of the heart. To meet the challenge and beat it, we have to deal with our psychology, the records of our karma, our will, and all of our desirings.

You can give yourself a life review right now. You don't have to wait till you cross to the other side. You can sit down today and write down what you think are your good deeds that have helped others. How have you gone out of your way? Are you so self-absorbed that you haven't even recognized that people need you and that you can give help to many, and so on? How much good karma will you have? Think about it.

If there are things that you don't like about yourself, you are in a position to change right now. I like to change every day. I like to transcend myself every day. I want to be more and more one with the angels. I want to be more and more godlike and not remain at the lower levels of the human consciousness. I don't want to waste my time. I want to accelerate because if I accelerate on the spiritual path, I can help others.

You can do the same. Make use of those moments. Go out and help people, especially the little children, especially our youth who are enmeshed in the astral, into satanic rituals and all kinds of things that really do give us pause as to what is happening in our world.

When we want God more than anything else in this universe, and when we can be still and know that the I AM Presence in us is God, we will not be moved from that center of the heart. I challenge you to try this on a daily basis and see what happens when you do not allow yourself to be moved by anything or anyone that comes your way.

You could keep a notebook on this—and you ought to if you're serious about it—because then you are kind of playing a game with yourself. You get a good grade if you resisted the momentums of depression or irritation or envy or whatever may be your weakness. And you notice when you don't. You notice when your energy descends. You notice what you eat, how it affects you, and how it takes you from your centeredness, and so forth. You become an observer of self. And you see how your devotions fuel your ability to change.

Light, Set Me Free!

We have come to establish and to reestablish the true nature of our being. We find that being within as the fiery core that we have defined as the OM and the I AM THAT I AM. Yet who can define and thus circumscribe consciousness that is God? We have touched upon the sacred Word that God has given of himself whereby, tracing the intonation of the sound and the joyous rays within our hearts, we might find the core of consciousness. When we touch the name of God, we touch the flame. When we touch the flame, we touch fohat—energy and light that will go forth in response to the spoken Word.

When you say a prayer with all the fire of your heart, it becomes a fiat, a command spoken with the authority of your individualized God Presence. As you meditate upon the words you say, realize that God himself is the fiat singing in your soul, coming forth with the power of the everlasting Word.

When we say, *"Light, set me free!"* we are speaking to that fiery core that is the OM, that is the I AM THAT I AM, that is the masculine-feminine polarity of being, the Father-Mother God. And we are giving a fiat: *Light, set me free! Light, set me free! Light, set me free!* Now, *light, command, command, command my being to be free! Light, demand my being free! Light, expand within my being!* Because this light I AM, I declare that *I AM that light!* I declare that *I AM a being of violet fire!* The violet fire proceeds out of the white-fire core. It is the flame of freedom which we will seize and run with. And finally, *I AM the purity God desires!*

In the OM, in the I AM THAT I AM, is God as being, as life desiring to be more being, more life, more consciousness. As we flow with that, as we impose our fiats of creation upon it, that fire expands from within. There is a certain expansion that takes place in meditation; but the mounting of the crescendo and the anchoring of the light in Matter, in molecules, in substance, in Terra, in earth, must come forth through the power of the spoken Word. This is why man, the co-creator with God, is given the power to utter speech. This is the sacred gift that enables us to make the spark of our divinity act in the physical plane.

Place your attention upon your heart and let the fire of creation go forth from your heart to the heart of God as you say this decree:

Light, Set Me Free!

Light, set me free!
Light, set me free!
Light, set me free!
Light command, light command,
    light command, command, command!
Light demand, light demand,
    light demand, demand, demand!
Light expand, light expand,
    light expand, expand, expand!
Light I AM, light I AM,
    light I AM, I AM, I AM!
I AM a being of violet fire,
I AM the purity God desires.

Freedom of Choice

You need to know yourself inside and out. But you are not that self. You are the point of light within. You are the soul that is gaining self-mastery, and you can be your Christ Self. Then you will not be moved by your four lower bodies or the attempts to break that wondrous love tryst that you have with your Holy Christ Self, with the angels, and with the ascended masters.

This is how you eliminate the risk in the calculation. The calculation of your life is that God put you here on earth and you will not be tempted except in matters where you have the momentum, the strength, the intelligence to beat that temptation, that illusion—if you want to.

So you see, it is not really a risk. But it takes all of your love and all of your striving and all of your determination. The flame you need is constancy. Don't be down one day and up the next. Keep steady. Not a flash in the pan, not a shooting star, but constant.

Ask yourself, "How am I living my life here on earth?" The object is to bring the heaven-world to earth as much as possible while not becoming materialists in the sense that we are so attached to the material world that we miss the victory we were intended to have over the material world.

This victory will give us the freedom of choice to be in the physical octave for a specific mission yet not subject to karma because we have balanced it. Therefore we will be able to serve life in a much greater role, and we will have the option of not returning to the physical plane but to contribute to the many evolutions of the cosmos that are evolving in the etheric octave.

What Will Your Next Life Be?

The ascended master Saint Germain has told us that we can earn our ascension in this life, or at the very least in our next life if there are karmic requirements that for some reason cannot be completed in this one. But he didn't say it would be easy. There are thirty-three initiations as well as a number of other requirements for the ascension. These requirements include not only balancing our karma and dissolving the densely packed negative records from previous lives in our electronic belt, but also balancing the God-power, God-wisdom, and God-love of our heart flame. It includes fulfilling our divine plan for our service to life, achieving mastery over the consciousness of outer conditions such as sickness and death, and much more. Does this sound daunting?

Early on I said that most of you will be returning for another life on earth because you will not yet have fulfilled your reason for being. But if you don't set your ascension as the goal of life, you may miss the mark in this life and future ones. If you shoot a basket, do you aim for "almost made it"? No! You focus on winning the game, even if it takes more than one shot.

Earth received a dispensation from the heavenly hierarchy in the early twentieth century whereby souls could take their ascension with only 51 percent of their karma balanced instead of the previous requirement of 100 percent. But how can you know how much karma you have balanced? The answer for most of us is that we don't know. And karma does not remain constant. It goes up and down moment by moment as we deal with the challenges of daily life.

The game of life demands a focus of creative tension—not anxiety, but a joyous spirit of victory that comes when you know deep down that you are worthy of winning. So don't feel overwhelmed by the requirements. Know that you have all the help you need available to you as you develop your relationship with the ascended masters and the angels. They will champion your cause and prep you for your ultimate victory—your graduation from the wheel of birth and rebirth. And from the day of your ascension, your "next life" will be lived in the etheric levels of heaven.

Graduation Rehearsal

Rehearsing is part of getting ready. The set of decrees I am giving to you here represent the steps, or stages, in the disciplines of the life of Jesus Christ, the same disciplines of all the saints of East and West who have graduated from this schoolroom of earth in the ritual of the ascension.*

The decrees begin with a meditation, drawing through the heart the energy that is the violet flame. We put our attention on the heart and use the power of visualization to see in our heart this violet flame of sacred fire of the Holy Spirit. Meditating upon the heart releases that energy through the heart.

> *Violet fire, thou love divine,*
> *Blaze within this heart of mine!*
> *Thou art mercy forever true,*
> *Keep me always in tune with you.*

Those four lines in rhyme represent an alchemical formula just like the matrix of a molecule, the atomic matrix of energy.

---

*To visualize yourself within the image of the Chart of Your Divine Self experiencing the action of these decrees and to hear them given by Elizabeth Clare Prophet, go to https://www.summitlighthouse.org/HHHvideo.

The visualization is for the drawing forth of the light of the I AM Presence and the anchoring of that light in the heart.

Always remember that it is not you giving the decree but God in you. God in you is the decree, the energy of the decree, the voice of the decree, and the person of the decree. Simply allow the free flow of your soul to move with that energy. It can be given once, three times, or a hundred times as you go deeper and deeper into meditation and visualization.

The science of the spoken Word activates the fruit of our meditation upon God and coalesces it in the physical plane. The decree begins the alchemical change. Alchemy is a method or power of transmutation, of transformation. And so as you use the science of the spoken Word, you may notice immediate physical changes in your life, physical changes in your body for health, changes in your mind for enlightenment, and also changes in the circumstances of your job, your home, your marriage, your family, and your children.

The next part of this set moves from the heart to focus on the head. We are seeking a balance of heart, head, and hand in this series of decrees as a balance of the action of the Trinity. So this is the decree for the head:

> *I AM light, thou Christ in me,*
> *Set my mind forever free;*
> *Violet fire, forever shine*
> *Deep within this mind of mine.*
>
> *God who gives my daily bread,*
> *With violet fire fill my head*
> *Till thy radiance heavenlike*
> *Makes my mind a mind of light.*

Now focusing on the hand:

> *I AM the hand of God in action,*
> *Gaining victory every day;*
> *My pure soul's great satisfaction*
> *Is to walk the Middle Way.*

As we give these mantras, we visualize the violet flame blazing through the heart and the head and then being released through the hand in action. The "Heart, Head and Hand" set of decrees is a ritual of the flow of energy. These decrees quiet the emotions. They integrate mind, body, and soul, and they are for the fulfillment of the self. They free the energies of life.

In the giving of these decrees, there is a clearing of records of centuries of incarnations. The subconscious mind is being cleared of those difficulties and problems that everyone has experienced that have caused the problems of psychosis and neurosis and all of the diseases to which we are heir. These decrees resolve patterns of consciousness. They develop a flow, an awareness, and an attunement with the Inner Self that makes for creativity—a feeling of being alive and well and in action for good on earth.

Tube of Light

The tube of light, which I gave you earlier, comes next in this series. It's a way of setting your forcefield for meditation, for the science of the spoken Word, or just for your daily activities. As a side note, get used to vocalizing your mantras and meditations. Doing this will increase their power in the physical octave. Try it out loud to see how it feels:

> *Beloved I AM Presence bright,*
> *Round me seal your tube of light*
> *From ascended master flame*
> *Called forth now in God's own name.*
> *Let it keep my temple free*
> *From all discord sent to me.*
>
> *I AM calling forth violet fire*
> *To blaze and transmute all desire,*
> *Keeping on in freedom's name*
> *Till I AM one with the violet flame.*

While giving this decree to the I AM Presence, you can visualize yourself standing inside this giant tube of light. And around you, see the energy of the violet flame saturating you, flowing through your body, blazing through the skin, through the arteries, the veins, the arms, the legs, the extremities. Feel this saturation of your being and concentrate on this vision of the Self.

That which you see, the energy you invoke, you will become. The energy of God will coalesce around your visualization and manifest according to the direction of your Inner Self, your Christ Self, who is always the director of the decree and the meditation.

Forgiveness

Affirming forgiveness puts us in tune with our Holy Christ Self, who has the authority within our being to forgive sin. In order to accept that forgiveness, we give the following decree:

> *I AM forgiveness acting here,*
> *Casting out all doubt and fear,*
> *Setting men forever free*
> *With wings of cosmic victory.*

I AM calling in full power
For forgiveness every hour;
To all life in every place
I flood forth forgiving grace.

As we forgive life, life forgives us. This mantra for forgiveness releases forgiveness to everyone. Wherever we have the sense of injustice or we have been wronged, we visualize this violet flame of forgiveness going forth from our heart. We visualize it contacting every individual with whom we have ever had a misunderstanding. And we feel a tremendous peace and love and a resolution of discord.

This is the law of the circle, the law of karma, the law of cause and effect, at work in our lives. When we sow energy as good vibration, we reap energy as good vibration, and we start an upward spiral. The culmination of that spiral is soul liberation whereby the soul reunites day by day with the Spirit of the living God. Through the science of the spoken Word we can be ascending a little more every day.

Abundance

Abundance is the natural law of life, to never want and yet not live in excess. This next decree is for our realization of this law of abundance.

I AM free from fear and doubt,
Casting want and misery out,
Knowing now all good supply
Ever comes from realms on high.
I AM the hand of God's own fortune
Flooding forth the treasures of light,
Now receiving full abundance
To supply each need of life.

This is an interesting decree because immediately we use the name of God, "I AM," and affirm our being free from fear and doubt. The basic cause of poverty is fear and doubt. We cannot draw forth abundance and supply if we have fear at conscious or subconscious levels.

When Jesus walked on the water, Peter asked if he could come and be on the water with his master. Jesus said, "Come," and Peter walked on the water. This transfer of energy came by Peter's attention upon Jesus, the Christ, and by Peter's belief. As long as he had his attention upon Jesus, Peter was above water. But when he momentarily entered into a vortex of his own fear, he immediately broke the contact and sank beneath the waves.

Jesus' body was filled with light, and that light overcame the natural laws of gravity. This was because of Jesus' own consciousness of perfection—he had the awareness of the Inner Master, the I AM Presence, as being perfect. But he did not hold that law of perfection as exclusive to himself. He taught that the law he demonstrated was available to everyone. Therefore he instructed us, "Be ye therefore perfect, even as your Father which is in heaven is perfect."

Perfection

This decree is to help us realize that we can entertain the law of perfection. God's energies of perfection can literally transform our lives.

> *I AM life of God-direction,*
> *Blaze thy light of truth in me.*
> *Focus here all God's perfection,*
> *From all discord set me free.*
>
> *Make and keep me anchored ever*
> *In the justice of thy plan—*

I AM the presence of perfection
Living the life of God in man!

So in our oneness with God, we can declare, "God in me is the life of God-direction." We can say, "God in me is the presence of perfection." And by cosmic law, it must manifest because we have combined it with the name of God, the all-power of a cosmos.

Transfiguration

With each successive decree in this series, you draw forth a greater degree of light. As you become more sensitive, you may begin to feel this light building within your body. You may begin to feel a greater burning of the flame within the heart.

This burning in the heart indicates the expansion of the threefold flame within your heart. The sacred fire is consuming misqualified energies of fear, hatred, and impure motives that often surround the heart. The one pursuing the initiation of the transfiguration, then, gives the following decree:

I AM changing all my garments,
Old ones for the bright new day;
With the sun of understanding
I AM shining all the way.

I AM light within, without;
I AM light is all about.
Fill me, free me, glorify me!
Seal me, heal me, purify me!
Until transfigured they describe me:
I AM shining like the Son,
I AM shining like the sun!

There is a tremendous joy in this decree because it represents an influx of light whereby the very cells of our bodies begin to be filled with light and to be flushed of physical as well as mental and emotional toxins. The joy of giving these decrees is the joy of becoming God.

Resurrection

Isn't it true that the last enemy to be overcome is death? The reality is that there is no death, but we have to prove it. The resurrection is a resurgence of God's energy through our being. Drawing forth the energies of the resurrection enabled Jesus to restore life to his body after the crucifixion. By the meditation of his soul upon his Christ Self, he overshadowed his body until he restored that body to life.

Now we begin our own resurrection by the restoration of consciousness, of joy, of happiness, of love, of truth. And we keep on increasing and accelerating God's consciousness within us until the ultimate victory over death is the natural conclusion of our soul's quest on the spiritual path—our soul's reunion with God. With this decree, you can say, "I am being resurrected every day! I am overcoming death every day!"

> *I AM the flame of resurrection*
> *Blazing God's pure light through me.*
> *Now I AM raising every atom,*
> *From every shadow I AM free.*
>
> *I AM the light of God's full Presence,*
> *I AM living ever free.*
> *Now the flame of life eternal*
> *Rises up to victory.*

Visualize white light coming through you, rising as a white fire pulsating from beneath your feet. It is an energy field that can restore you from sickness to health, from depression to wholeness, from anxiety to joy.

We give the decree on the resurrection to remove the consciousness of death. More than we realize, we are burdened by the energies of death on a day-to-day basis. Fear is the beginning of death. Doubt in oneself is the beginning of death. The condemnation or the belittlement of the self is the murdering of the self and its potential to be free. Freedom comes through this resurrection flame.

Death is only real to those who believe that our life is actually limited to the body. But life is in the flame in the heart and in the soul, and these move on as the path of acceleration continues here and hereafter.

Ascension

After the resurrection comes the ascension. The ascension is the acceleration of consciousness. It is actually the increase of the vibratory rate of the electrons as they whirl about and through the nucleus of the atom until ultimately the soul reunites with the I AM Presence, the individualized Presence of God.

This is the concluding decree in this series. As soon as we begin to give it, we are accelerating the white light in our auras, preparing for that ultimate reunion with God at the conclusion of this life or at the conclusion of a future life, perhaps even our next incarnation.

I AM ascension light,
Victory flowing free,
All of good won at last
For all eternity.

I AM light, all weights are gone.
Into the air I raise;
To all I pour with full God-power
My wondrous song of praise.

All hail! I AM the living Christ,
The ever-loving One.
Ascended now with full God-power,
I AM a blazing sun!

The visualization for this decree is a sphere of white light that now envelops your entire form, your entire being. When you say, "I AM the living Christ," you are affirming, "God in me is the living Christ, and that Christ which was in Jesus and in all the saints and masters of East and West is now manifesting in me as the fullness of the threefold flame in my heart."

The goal of immortality is something that is near and dear to the people of every religion in the world. Whether it's called soul liberation or the ascension or nirvana, it is the same thing. The ascension is our acceleration of the consciousness of God within us and our return to the white-fire core of being, the core of consciousness. Christians call it going to heaven and Buddhists call it entering parinirvana, the great soul liberation. It is indeed liberation. It is our freedom from the rounds of rebirth and our freedom from our own karma.

I really think that the awareness that we can return to God in this life is something many do not have. Others have a misconception of it; they think that by a simple declaration of faith or confession of the name Jesus Christ they will automatically be received into the courts of heaven. Unfortunately this is not so, for the law of karma requires that we balance every jot and tittle of karma. And so God has provided for us the way of reincarnation whereby the soul comes back again and again until at last she can finally prove the law of love and reunite with the living God.

Who Is Serapis?

Serapis Bey serves as the chohan of the fourth ray, as you can see in the chart on page 210, Appendix A. His retreat is The Temple of the Ascension, over Luxor, Egypt, where he prepares candidates for the ascension.

Serapis says, "I think that those who think they cannot be perfect imagine that perfection is a straitjacket or a sterile quality lacking any verve or energy or joy or spontaneity. Nay, perfection is the flowering of the lilies, of the gentle violets. Perfection is a smile upon a face.

"God does not measure perfection by human standards. After all, how can the human have a standard of perfection? God measures the motive in the heart, the love in the heart. And that which mankind criticize, God ennobles as perfection. . . .

"We need not complicate cosmic law. Cosmic law is love in action. Cosmic love is law in action. Cosmic love and law are your faith, your hope, your joy. . . .

"And if you could see all that heaven holds in store for you, you would be swift and take the wings of the eagles to fly into our retreats in the highest crannies of the mountains. You would come, you would run from your earthly involvements."[2]

....

The ascended master Serapis Bey teaches that the path of the ascension is the path of love, the dream of love fulfilled. So we know that it is the way of love that leads to the way of purity and eventually to the ascension. Those who have ascended have come from every continent and through every religion, but all have achieved that ascension through the disciplines of love. As Serapis says, "The disciplines for the initiations of the ascension into higher consciousness can be borne only by love—by the heart and the soul so filled with love for God, the Great Guru, that it will endure unto the end, the end of the cycles of human consciousness."[3]

The Karmic Labyrinth

Our job on earth is to balance our karma and make the world the best place it can possibly be. We can leave footprints in the sands of time that say, "There is another schoolroom, a heaven-world at etheric levels where you can fulfill more of your reason for being and all of your dreams. There is no end to opportunity once you balance your karma. You can be once again with your twin flame—your masculine or feminine counterpart who was conceived out of the same white-fire body, the fiery ovoid of the I AM Presence—and with all those souls who are a part of your evolution."

Keeping the goal of getting to the etheric levels and the ultimate goal of your ascension before you is like having a treasure map. But the labyrinth of karma is an illusion to keep you from ever reaching for that shining city in the etheric. You cannot perfect something that doesn't have the capacity to contain perfection. Neither the astral plane nor the physical plane has the capacity to contain perfection, but perfection can and does exist in the etheric octave.

If you want to live permanently in the etheric octave and in all of the beautiful places that people have seen in near-death experiences, you must have woven the deathless solar garment, the deathless solar body. It is called the wedding garment. This "wedding" is the wedding of your soul to your Higher Self, the living Christ. To enter into that octave of the etheric plane, you must have that sheath of light around you that is the wedding garment.

At this point you need the ascended masters more than you know. You need a teacher to guide you, precisely at the point that you believe you are secure in your adaptation to the planes of illusion and need no one—nothing except the clever mind of your lower self, the most clever of all fellows you know! Bound to the wheel of rebirth into and out of a smug, self-satisfied existence, you are in danger of violating the laws of God unknowingly. And you have no guarantee that you will reincarnate midst enlightened ones who will lead you out of your karmic labyrinth.

Finding the Masters

This is a true story about someone who found her way to the ascended masters. A young woman had a near-death experience after a car accident. When she woke up in the hospital, she could not remember the accident. All she could remember was the following:

> I just remember flying through this vacuum. It was like a dark darkness, and it was a void. I actually could not put it into words myself until later when I read Raymond Moody's book *Life After Life*. It felt like I was flying through something with these bright, bright lights just coming at me. And then I just came out into this peaceful place.
>
> I don't remember any background. I just remember standing before this beautiful being that I thought of as God. The form it took was that of a loving, older man. I think it took the form that I needed to see.
>
> I was raised . . . with the fear and the guilt and all that. I had turned pretty much into an atheist. I knew that I really believed in God, but through those teenage years my parents didn't get along and things were pretty rough for me. I just turned really resentful towards God. I didn't believe that there was anything out there. I thought God wouldn't make a world like this.
>
> It was such a brilliant, bright light. It felt like the essence of that image was this light. He kept saying over and over the words: "Are you prepared to die?"
>
> When I woke up and I laid in that hospital, I just kept hearing those words, "Are you prepared to die?" He wasn't actually speaking them. Everything was a vibration. What he was showing me was that I was a part of him and I was a part of that light and my soul was a drop out of the ocean. I was a part of God and God had given me light, and

I could take this light and do whatever I pleased with it.

He showed me what I had been doing with the light and asked me if I was prepared to die and if I had accomplished what I wanted to accomplish in this life. I felt so much gratitude for being shown that what I was doing was not worthwhile. I had the feeling of begging to go back and to really do something with my life.

I did a complete turnaround. I wanted to really center my life around God. All I wanted to do was to find out what life is all about.

After her experience, this young woman began actively searching. Her search led her through more than one spiritual activity. Finally, she found Kuthumi and Djwal Kul's book on the human aura.[4] She said that what told her the teachings were right was the focus on the light of God and the I AM Presence.

There was something in that book that I recognized. Just the purity of the teaching. Every other group that I had gotten into either they used the teachings to help you get money or to advance yourself in a selfish way. But this was the first thing I found that was for the good of your soul and would raise you up to a higher level. And that was the thing that I was shown by God, that you have to keep raising yourself to a higher level in order to reach the level where you can be with God. And that's what I was searching for.

The Priceless Thread of Contact

When you make contact with the ascended masters, the thread of contact is established. If you choose to pursue the teachings of the ascended masters and a spiritual path, that thread of contact gets stronger and stronger until it is a veritable rope. And then it becomes like a steel cable. And you never let go of the ascended masters and the heavenly hosts lifetime after lifetime until you make it Home.

It is very important to nourish the flame of that contact and to hold onto it, because there are times in one's experience when that contact with the ascended masters is your life preserver and the most important thing you have. And one of those times is when you are passing from this physical octave and from this body at the time of your transition.

Remember, there are some things of ultimate importance in your life. All of the passing fancies of life, all of the possessions that we can fascinate ourselves with, all of the new this and the new that don't go with you. Everybody else gets those physical things and you go naked as a soul back to God. And at that moment, the most priceless possession you have is the thread of contact with those elder brothers and sisters who can assist you in your journey.

So greet each day joyfully, knowing that you have the ascended masters as your teachers, that you can rise with the violet flame, balance your daily allotment of karma, and spiral higher and higher even while you abide on earth. By bringing a bit of heaven to earth every step of the way, the very essence of life on earth will change. We truly are the change we want to see if we are on the homeward path yet tarry to help, to teach, and to offer compassion to anyone in need while we are here.

Time is precious. Life is precious. Treasure this opportunity you have been given to be alive on earth and make the most of it.

May you win all the way!

Elizabeth Clare Prophet

Spiritual Retreats

The seven color rays are the natural division of the pure white light from the heart of God as it descends through the prism of manifestation. These seven rays represent seven paths to eventually achieve your union with God in the ritual of the ascension. The lord, or chohan, of each ray teaches the way of self-mastery to those who desire to expand particular God-qualities.

Ask to be taken in your etheric body while you sleep at night to study in these spiritual retreats:

> *In the name of Almighty God and my own Higher Self, I call to beloved Archangel Michael and your blue lightning angels to protect and take me in my etheric body while I sleep to the spiritual retreat of* [master's name]. *I gratefully accept this done according to God's will.*

RAY	COLOR	MASTER	RETREAT
1-Power	Blue	El Morya	Darjeeling, India

While on earth, a statesman, poet, economist, and saint. Teaches the understanding of the will of God and the divine blueprint, or plan, for your soul. Works with those in positions of leadership, organizers, community leaders, holders of public office, and those involved with international relations.

2-Wisdom	Yellow	Lanto	Grand Teton, Wyoming

Oversees all systems of education and institutions of higher learning and is concerned with the illumination of the youth of the world. Interprets ancient wisdom in a practical way for the Western mind and facilitates the New Age path for Eastern traditionalists. Works with teachers, philosophers, and educators.

3-Love	Pink	Paul the Venetian	Southern France

Divine artist conferring by the excellence of works the image of Christ unique to every soul, preparing them by love's disciplines for higher spiritual initiations. Works with artists, designers, and all those who desire to bring forth the beauty of the culture of the ascended masters on earth.

4-Purity	White	Serapis Bey	Luxor, Egypt

Receives and trains candidates for the ascension. Architect of holy orders, the inner life, and golden-age cities, and military disciplinarian of the forces of light, peace, and freedom. Works with architects, planners, and those dedicated to the purity and discipline of any undertaking.

5-Truth	Green	Hilarion	Crete, Greece

Teacher of all physical and metaphysical branches of science and the healing arts. Works with atheists, agnostics, skeptics, and others who have been disillusioned with life and with religion. Also works with scientists, healers, musicians, mathematicians, and all those who pursue truth.

6-Service	Purple & Gold with Ruby	Nada	Saudi Arabia

Advocate of souls before the Karmic Board and unifier of families and twin flames. Teaches mastery of the emotions and the practical application of love through service to life. Works with ministers, nurses, psychologists, counselors at law, public servants, and all who administer to the needs of humanity.

7-Freedom	Violet	Saint Germain	Romania

Sponsor of the United States of America and hierarch of the Aquarian age. Alchemist of the sacred fire who gave us the gift of the violet flame of freedom for transmutation of individual and world karma. Works with diplomats, actors, writers, defenders of freedom, and priests/priestesses of the sacred fire.

"I Didn't Think You Were Supposed to Be Able to Talk to God"

After practicing for twenty years, Dr. Melvin Morse retired from the full-time practice of pediatrics. He then became the Research Director of the Institute for the Scientific Study of Consciousness (ISSC). While Director of ISSC, he was awarded the Warcollier International Prize for consciousness research. Morse has appeared on radio and television programs to discuss his extensive research on NDEs in children. He has written five books, including *Closer to the Light* and *Transformed by the Light*.

On December 14, 2018, Morse shared an article in a series called *Better Understanding Consciousness Through Children's NDEs*.

Morse opens the article by saying, "Sometimes the accounts of near-death experiences themselves contain elements which prove that they are 'real,' meaning that we can trust the information gained from them." He personally resuscitated Jamie, the eight-year-old girl whose story he tells from the context of his professional medical and scientific experience. He also verified that she was indeed clinically dead during the time she witnessed details of the operating room and met someone she thought was Jesus. "He was very nice," she said. She also saw a light which told her "who she was and where she was to go." She also met "grandpas, grammas, and babies waiting to be born."

The following is excerpted from his article "I Didn't Think You Were Supposed to Be Able to Talk to God."[1]

> Jamie was rushed to Valley Medical Center in Renton, Washington by her private physician after she went into a coma in his office. She had a form of bacterial brain infection which should have resulted in death within a few hours of presentation. Instead she lived to draw a picture of her own resuscitation. . . .
>
> Our research team interviewed her several months after her cardiac arrest as part of our study of survivors of cardiac arrest in the Intensive Care Unit at Seattle Children's Hospital. She had not told anyone of her experience. When I asked her why she hadn't told anyone, she whispered to me, "I didn't think that you were supposed to be able to talk to God."
>
> How can we believe this story? Jamie comes from a Lutheran family who is not particularly religious. The Jesus that she describes looks more like Santa Claus than the typical Jesus portrayed in the pictures in her household and at her church. Her church and family do not teach reincarnation, nor do they say that there is a door in heaven where babies waiting to be born return to, as I saw in the bottom right hand corner of [her] drawing. Jamie drew me [a] picture of her cardiac resuscitation and ascension to heaven several months after her successful recovery from clinical death.
>
> By clinical death, I mean that her heart had stopped beating, she was not breathing on her own, and she was in a profound coma which prevented her from seeing or hearing anything through her ordinary senses. Her brain was on

the edge of complete cellular death from which there can be no recovery. In the state of clinical death, patients are not dreaming; they have little brain activity and lack the ability to create complex hallucinations such as those described in the typical near-death experience. Their brain is not functioning at all; it is completely shut down. . . .

We understand that the brain is shutting down to preserve the integrity of its cellular structure. The brain at the end of life tries to conserve energy and oxygenation to its cells. If the near-death experience is a hallucination, then it must involve almost all of various areas of the brain, including the visual cortex, hearing cortex, language centers and emotions. This is unlikely to be occurring in an otherwise dysfunctional dying brain. . . .

There are three important details which document for me that Jamie was fully conscious and witnessed her own resuscitation. First, she draws me wearing a hat at the head of the bed. This is not a detail she could have invented from watching resuscitations on television. Secondly, she draws my partner Dr. Christopher with his arms and hands in perfect position for cardiac compressions. Again, this is a detail it is unlikely that an 8-year-old child would invent. Finally, below her bed, she clearly draws the crash cart used for cardiac resuscitation. Again, a seemingly minor detail that has profound significance.

Her dying dysfunctional brain could not have invented these details. Her eyes were taped shut to protect them as she had no blink reflex, so she could not have seen any of these details by ordinary means. There simply is no scientific explanation for the . . . drawing with its accurate details except that her consciousness existed outside of her body during her resuscitation.

She is not the only patient who has provided me with

details that prove that their near-death experiences were real. One young girl who nearly drowned told me that she was told in heaven that she had to return to earth to help her mother with a child as yet unborn who had heart disease. She told me this prior to the birth of her brother, who turned out to have heart disease. I had a patient once who laughingly told me that he saw us trying to cardiovert him with paddles only to realize that the machine became unplugged from the wall. In fact that did happen during his ultimately successful resuscitation. . . .

These are patients that I resuscitated and interviewed, so I directly know that the events are true. However, when these stories are told and retold and are heard through second- and third-hand accounts, there is a legitimate concern that the stories might be embellished or even fabricated. In twenty-five years of studying these experiences, I have encountered a handful of fabricated experiences. Usually they are unwitting or unconscious fabrications without an intent to deceive, although that happens as well.

Science begins with observations. That is where we are now in our exploration of the science of the near-death experience. We have credible observations by children of their own resuscitations and of a spiritual existence that awaits us all after death. These do not seem to be inventions of the mind after recovery from near death but rather [they] contain details which indicate that they occur in the final moments of life, just as the children say that they do.

Carl G. Jung's Near-Death Experience

Carl Gustav Jung (July 26, 1875–June 6, 1961) was a Swiss psychologist and psychiatrist who pioneered analytic psychology, emphasizing the individual psyche and the personal quest for wholeness. He developed the concepts of extraversion and introversion, archetypes, and the collective unconscious.

In a Swiss hospital in 1944, Jung had a near-death experience after a heart attack. He recorded what he saw as well as his own thoughts and feelings about life and death. Jung had a very rich background in the spiritual traditions and cultures of the world, and naturally his experience was born of that. Yet there is much to savor in his story and to consider in your contemplation of what this book has explored.

The following is a portion of Jung's fascinating experience as he tells it in his autobiographical work, *Memories, Dreams, Reflections.*[1]

> At the beginning of 1944 I broke my foot, and this misadventure was followed by a heart attack. In a state of unconsciousness I experienced deliriums and visions which must have begun when I hung on the edge of death and was

being given oxygen and camphor injections. The images were so tremendous that I myself concluded that I was close to death. My nurse afterward told me, "It was as if you were surrounded by a bright glow." That was a phenomenon she had sometimes observed in the dying, she added. I had reached the outermost limit, and do not know whether I was in a dream or an ecstasy. At any rate, extremely strange things began to happen to me.

It seemed to me that I was high up in space. Far below I saw the globe of the earth, bathed in a gloriously blue light. I saw the deep blue sea and the continents. . . . I knew that I was on the point of departing from the earth. . . .

After a period of contemplating the amazing view while he was floating through space high above the earth, Jung noticed a block of stone as large as his house also floating in space.

An entrance led into a small antechamber. . . . Two steps led up to this antechamber, and inside, on the left, was the gate to the temple. Innumerable tiny niches, each with a saucer-like concavity filled with coconut oil and small burning wicks, surrounded the door with a wreath of bright flames. . . .

Everything I aimed at or wished for or thought . . . fell away or was stripped from me—an extremely painful process. Nevertheless something remained; it was as if I now carried along with me everything I had ever experienced or done, everything that had happened around me. . . . I consisted of my own history and I felt with great certainty: this is what I am. . . .

This experience gave me a feeling of extreme poverty, but at the same time of great fullness. There was no longer anything I wanted or desired. I existed in an objective form;

I was what I had been and lived. At first the sense of annihilation predominated, of having been stripped or pillaged; but suddenly that became of no consequence. . . .

Something else engaged my attention: As I approached the temple, I had the certainty that I was about to enter an illuminated room and would meet there all those people to whom I belong in reality. There I would at last understand—this too was a certainty—what historical nexus I or my life fitted into. I would know what had been before me, why I had come into being, and where my life was flowing. My life as I lived it had often seemed to me like a story that has no beginning and no end. I had the feeling that I was a historical fragment, an excerpt for which the preceding and succeeding text was missing. My life seemed to have been snipped out of a long chain of events, and many questions had remained unanswered. Why had it taken this course? Why had I brought these particular assumptions with me? What had I made of them? What will follow? I felt sure that I would receive an answer to all these questions as soon as I entered the rock temple. There I would meet the people who knew the answer to my question about what had been before and what would come after.

But Jung, as so many others who have had NDEs, found that he was to return to earth.

I was profoundly disappointed, for now it all seemed to have been for nothing. The painful process of defoliation had been in vain, and I was not to be allowed to enter the temple, to join the people in whose company I belonged.

In reality, a good three weeks were still to pass before I could truly make up my mind to live again. I could not eat because all food repelled me. . . . Disappointed, I thought:

"Now I must return to 'the box system' again." For it seemed to me as if behind the horizon of the cosmos a three-dimensional world had been artificially built up, in which each person sat by himself in a little box. And now I should have to convince myself all over again that this was important! Life and the whole world struck me as a prison. . . . While I floated in space, I had been weightless, and there had been nothing tugging at me. And now all that was to be a thing of the past!

Gradually he began to reclaim his renewed opportunity on earth and found his near-death experience to have enhanced his ability to achieve his goals.

After the illness, a fruitful period of work began for me. A good many of my principal works were written only then. The insight I had had, or the vision of the end of all things, gave me the courage to undertake new formulations. I no longer attempted to put across my own opinion but surrendered myself to the current of my thoughts. Thus one problem after the other revealed itself to me and took shape. . . .

It was only after the illness that I understood how important it is to affirm one's own destiny. In this way we forge an ego that does not break down when incomprehensible things happen; an ego that endures, that endures the truth, and that is capable of coping with the world and with fate. Then, to experience defeat is also to experience victory. Nothing is disturbed—neither inwardly nor outwardly, for one's own continuity has withstood the current of life and of time. But that can come to pass only when one does not meddle inquisitively with the workings of fate."

NOTES

Chapter 2   WHAT HAPPENS WHEN PEOPLE DIE

1. Melvin Morse with Paul Perry, *Closer to the Light: Learning from Children's Near-Death Experiences* (New York: Villard Books, 1994), pp. 99–102.

2. Melvin Morse with Paul Perry, *Parting Visions: Uses and Meaning of Pre-Death, Psychic, and Spiritual Experiences* (New York: Villard Books, 1994), pp. 79–81. Morse, *Closer to the Light,* pp. 109–111.

3. Raymond A. Moody with Paul Perry, *The Light Beyond* (New York: Bantam, 1988), p. 43.

4. Raymond A. Moody, *Reflections on Life After Life* (New York: Bantam, 1977), pp. 17–18.

5. Moody, *The Light Beyond,* p. 13.

6. Ibid., p. 13.

7. Ibid., p. 14.

8. Ibid., p. 14.

9. Raymond A. Moody, *Life After Life* (New York: Bantam, 1976), p. 65.

10. Ibid., pp. 89, 92.

11. Moody, *The Light Beyond,* pp. 35–36.

12. Moody, *Life After Life,* pp. 97–98.

13. Ibid., p. 143.

14. Moody, *Reflections,* p. 19.

15. Ibid., p. 20.
16. Ibid., p. 21.
17. Ibid., p. 22.
18. Ibid., p. 18.
19. Angie Fenimore, interview by Elizabeth Clare Prophet on "Heart to Heart," WALE Talk Radio 990, September 22, 1997.

Chapter 3 WHAT ARE YOUR AFTERLIFE OPTIONS

1. *The Mahatma Letters to A. P. Sinnett,* A. Trevor Barker, transcriber and compiler (Pasadena, CA: Theosophical University Press, 1975), p. 101.
2. Min Bahadur Shakya, *Buddhist Himalaya: A Journal of Nagarjuna Institute of Exact Methods,* vol. IX, no. I & II (1998), "Smaller Sukhavati Vyuha Sutra," 2–2, 3. (http://enlight.lib.ntu.edu.tw/FULLTEXT/JR-BH/bh117552.htm)
3. Bhikshu Sangharakshita, *A Survey of Buddhism* (Boulder, CO: Shambhala Publications, 1980), p. 334.
4. Clare Ansbury, "The Free-Form Funeral," *Wall Street Journal,* March 2, 2019. (https://www.wsj.com/articles/the-free-form-funeral-11551542400?mod=e2fb&fbclid=IwAR37TguMXXR6hv2Kpqk-tVC8aIpMYAWpbaLmFUwTazvycCfj_T9eeU12Qz4)
5. Originating from Book VI of *Plato's Republic,* "ship of fools" refers to an allegory about a ship with a dysfunctional crew.
6. To hear "I AM Light," go to https://www.summitlighthouse.org/LightAudio.

Chapter 4 THE DANGERS OF DISCARNATES

1. *Ghost* is a 1990 American romantic fantasy thriller film directed by Jerry Zucker, written by Bruce Joel Rubin. *Ghost* was theatrically released on July 13, 1990 by Paramount Pictures.

Chapter 5 TAKING HEAVEN BY FORCE

1. *Flatliners* is a 1990 movie directed by Joel Schumacher, screenplay by Peter Filardi. This analysis is of the original movie, which was later remade with a different script. Rated R, it has some graphic sexuality and very dark gothic content. But even if you haven't seen this movie, the spiritual points made in this book are important ones and can be understood through the descriptions given.

Chapter 6 COMMANDING THE LIGHT

1. *Pearls of Wisdom,* vol. 28, no. 37, Lanello, August 27, 1995.

2. Isa. 45:11.

3. In December 2018, the *Wall Street Journal* ran an article giving grisly detail about Latin America, which has the highest murder rate in the world. "With little faith in the police or the courts to bring criminals to justice, mobs routinely kill suspected lawbreakers in spontaneous attacks." Violent "justice" was cited in Peru, Bolivia, Mexico, and Brazil. Not even 20 percent of the murders are solved in this general region.

   Brazil's economic recession has caused police protection and the legal system to lag far behind community needs. In Latin America, some public lynchings and torture have been sparked over the messaging service WhatsApp. Sadly, some victims have been innocent.

   "In a society haunted by violence, lynchings are cathartic acts meant to reimpose order," said an author on extralegal justice in Latin America and adviser to the U.N. on the issue. But she admitted that these mass attacks "only create more injustice, and more insecurity."

   Some evangelical churches believe that locals of one area are "possessed by the devil" because lynching has become so common. A missionary said, "They said they couldn't stop themselves . . . until they saw the blood."

These types of crime, wherever they occur across the world, are typical of possession by mass entities.

(Samantha Pearson and Luciana Magalhaes, "In Latin America, Awash in Crime, Citizens Impose Their Own Brutal Justice," *Wall Street Journal,* December 6, 2018. https://www.wsj.com/articles/in-a-continent-awash-in-crime-citizens-impose-their-own-brutal-justice-1544110959)

4. A May 30, 2018, *New York Times* article, "For 'Columbiners,' School Shootings Have a Deadly Allure," said that after the mass shooting in Santa Fe, New Mexico, researchers recognized but were not able to explain this: "The mass shootings that are now occurring with disturbing regularity at the nation's schools are shocking, disturbing, tragic—and seemingly contagious."

    The seemingly contagious violence has begun branching off Columbine, researchers say, and is now bringing in more recent attacks, many of them building off the details and media fixation with the last. School gunmen have admitted to investigators that they were now effectively competing with other attackers, in trying to come up with deadlier tactics, and in trying to kill the most people.

    "The phenomenon is feeding on itself," said Peter Langman, a psychologist who is the author of *Why Kids Kill: Inside the Minds of School Shooters* and who runs the website School Shooters.info. "It's gaining momentum, and the more there are, the more there will be." (Manny Fernandez, Julie Turkewitz, and Jess Bidgood, *New York Times,* May 30, 2018. https://www.nytimes.com/2018/05/30/us/school-shootings-columbine.html)

    This underscores the need for the spiritual work to be done. Our school personnel, psychologists, and law enforcement are doing their best, but the mass entities on the astral plane that feed this kind of crime must be dealt with at the spiritual level.

5. If you are interested in reading more about Archangel Michael, see the *Archangel Michael* pocket guide at https://www.sum mitlighthouse.org/ArchangelMichael-AL.

6. Moody, *The Light Beyond,* p. 151.

7. Mark L. Prophet and Elizabeth Clare Prophet, *Morya and You: Wisdom* (Gardiner, MT: Summit University Press, 2019), p. 80.

8. The movie industry, through extremely violent and bizarre material, has drawn an often unhealthy stream of followers in subcultures. Certain particularly gruesome movies have been called "cult classics."

    Online, IMDb wrote up the plot of *Copycat Killers,* which began in 2016, saying:

    "We all love seeing movies—some people turn the fun into an obsession! *Copycat Killers* is a true crime TV series that tells stories of real crimes that were inspired by major motion pictures and television. These real killers bring the violence of the movies into the real world, telling tales more shocking than what we see on screen. . . . The real life crime, including the killer's chilling back-story, the murders, and the exciting investigation, is shown as a parallel to the Hollywood hit. Featuring dramatic recreations and detailed insights from detectives, psychologists, film critics, and other experts, *Copycat Killers* tells these terrifying true stories that'll change the way you see movies." (https://www.imdb.com/title/tt5545018/ plotsummary)

    In September 2017, Ray Surette, *Oxford Research Encyclopedias: Criminology and Criminal Justice,* posted an article that said:

    "Copycat crime has traditionally been conceived within an emphasis on direct exposure to live person-to-person models. The media as a source of crime models has historically been downplayed. As the media evolved in the 20th century the study of mediated copycat crime models ascended so that the dominant contemporary view of copycat crime is that of media-sourced transmissions. Copycat crimes are today linked to literature, movies, television shows, music, video games, and print and television news, but despite concern and a large number of studies of violent media's relationship to social aggression, the rigorous study of copycat crime has lagged." (https://oxfordre.com/criminology/view/10.1093/acrefore /978 0190264079.001.0001/acrefore-9780190264079-e-33)

9. *Pearls of Wisdom,* vol. 38, no. 38, Jesus Christ, September 3, 1995.

10. *Crux,* an online Catholic news source reported that after the 2015 shooting at Umpqua Community College in Oregon, which caused the death of ten students, a priest began leading his parish in what they call the "Prayer to St. Michael" after daily Mass. In fall 2018, there appears to have been an uptick in pastors and bishops across the United States asking parishioners to recite this prayer together at the end of Mass, partly in response to the Catholic Church abuse crisis. However, a number of Catholics have given it since they were young. One who served in the Marine Corps said that he had given this prayer daily, and sometimes more often during active duty, and giving it now "reminds him of what spiritual life requires." (Carol Zimmermann, "Prayer to St. Michael Makes Resurgence in Response to Abuse Crisis," *Crux,* October 4, 2018. https: //cruxnow.com/church-in-the-usa/2018/10/04/prayer-to-st-michael- makes-resurgence-in-response-to-abuse-crisis/)

Another *Crux* article says: "Believers recognize that when Michael is called, he comes fiercely and mightily.... Prayer is a powerful thing. It should not be underestimated.... As his presence is sought, we have to be ready for him to expose and fight even against the evil within ourselves and within the leadership of our Church." (Father Jeffrey F. Kirby, "With the Archangel Prayer, Be Careful What You Wish For," *Crux,* October 14, 2018. https://cruxnow.com/commentary/2018/10/14/ with-the-archangel-prayer-be-careful-what-you-wish-for/)

Archangels do not belong to any particular church or religion, nor do they require your membership in order for you to ask them for help. The more people of any spiritual persuasion that give this prayer with all the fire of their hearts, the more change we may see in ourselves and in the world for the better!

11. Rev. 20:15.

Chapter 7   REINCARNATION: WHAT YOU NEED TO KNOW

1. Claire Gecewicz, "'New Age' beliefs common among both religious and nonreligious Americans," *Pew Research Center,* October 1, 2018. (https://www.pewresearch.org/fact-tank/2018 /10/01/new-age-beliefs-common-among-both-religious-and-nonreli gious-americans/)

2. See *Reincarnation: The Missing Link in Christianity* at https:// www.summitlighthouse.org/ReincarnationLink.

3. Elizabeth Clare Prophet, *Nine Cats and Nine Lives: Karma, Reincarnation and You,* DVDs available at https://www.sum mitlighthouse.org/NineLives.

4. Elizabeth Clare Prophet begins with a paraphrased version of "The Hymn of the Pearl" and explores the journey of our souls through the continuum of time, life, death, and reincarnation in *The Story of Your Soul: Recovering the Pearl of Your True Identity.* (https://www.summitlighthouse.org/SoulStory) The quote is taken from "The Hymn of the Pearl" (The Hymn of Judas Thomas the Apostle in the Country of the Indians), translated by G.R.S. Mead. (gnosis.org/library/hymnpearl.htm)

5. *Prie-dieu* (French). A kneeling bench fitted with a raised shelf on which the elbows or a book may be rested, designed for use by a person at prayer.

6. See the book *Hilarion the Healer* at https://www.summitlight house.org/HilarionHealer.

7.   Mark L. Prophet and Elizabeth Clare Prophet, *Lords of the Seven Rays* (Gardiner, MT: Summit University Press, 1986), pp. 549–550.

8.   Elizabeth Clare Prophet, *Saint Germain: Master Alchemist* (Corwin Springs, MT: Summit University Press, 2004), pp. 13–15, 17, emphasis added. (https://www.summitlighthouse.org/ SaintGermain-AL)

9.   Prophet, *Lords of the Seven Rays,* p. 551.

Chapter 8   INTEGRATING IT ALL

1.   I Cor. 15:41.

2.   Serapis Bey, *Dossier on the Ascension,* (Gardiner, MT: Summit University Press, 1995), "The Sensings of Serapis," p. 6 prior to title page.

3.   Prophet, *Lords of the Seven Rays,* p. 389.

4.   The most recent edition of the book mentioned in this true story is Kuthumi and Djwal Kul, *The Human Aura* (Gardiner, MT: Summit University Press, 2015). (https://www.summitlight house.org/TheHumanAura)

Appendix B

1.   Melvin Morse, "I Didn't Think You Were Supposed to Be Able to Talk to God," *The University of Heaven,* December 14, 2018. (https://www.theuniversityofheaven.com/blog/i-didn-t-think-you-were-supposed-to-be-able-to-talk-to-god)

Appendix C

1.   C. G. Jung, *Memories, Dreams, Reflections,* recorded and edited by Aniela Jaffe, translated from German by Richard and Clara Winston (New York: Vintage Books, 1989), pp. 289–297.

Glossary

Ascended masters. Those souls who have mastered time and space and in the process gained the mastery in their four lower bodies, in the four quadrants of Matter, and in their chakras. Ascended masters have also balanced at least 51 percent of their karma, balanced their threefold flame, fulfilled their divine plan, and taken the initiations of the ritual of the ascension. Ascended masters inhabit the planes of Spirit (God's consciousness). As well as having taught by the example of their lives on earth, they may teach unascended souls in an etheric temple or in cities of the heaven-world. By following the spiritual path, you, too, can become an ascended master!

Ascension. The ritual whereby the soul reunites with the Spirit of the living God, the I AM Presence, through the acceleration of the sacred fire at the victorious conclusion of her final lifetime on earth. Having met all requirements for the ascension, the soul, as the bride of Christ, merges first with her Christ consciousness and then with the living Presence of the I AM THAT I AM. After the ascension, the soul is then free from the rounds of karma and rebirth.

Astral plane. A frequency of time and space beyond the physical corresponding with the emotional body of humanity and the collective unconscious. It is the repository of humanity's thoughts and feelings, conscious and unconscious. Although intended to be for the amplification of the pure feelings of God, the astral plane has been muddied by impure thought and feeling. Thus the term "astral" is often used in a negative context to refer to that which is impure.

Bodhisattva. Sanskrit, "a being of bodhi or enlightenment." One whose energy and power is directed toward enlightenment, a bodhisattva is destined to become the Buddha but has forgone the bliss of nirvana with a vow to save all beings on earth. Two of the primary qualities of a bodhisattva are kindness and fearless compassion.

Buddha. Sanskrit, "awake, know, perceive"; "the enlightened one." An office in the spiritual hierarchy of the heaven-world that is attained by passing certain initiations of the sacred fire, including those of the seven rays of the Holy Spirit and of the five secret rays, and the raising of the feminine ray (sacred fire of the Kundalini).

Causal body. Interpenetrating spheres of light surrounding each soul's I AM Presence at spiritual levels. These spheres contain the records of all virtuous acts performed during the soul's many incarnations on earth to the glory of God rather than to the glory of the human ego.

Chakra. Sanskrit, "wheel, disc, circle." An energy center of light anchored in the etheric body that governs the flow of energy to one's four lower bodies. There are seven major chakras corresponding to the seven rays, five minor chakras corresponding to the five secret rays, and a total of 144 light centers corresponding to certain points of the physical body.

Chohan. Tibetan, "lord, master." Each of the seven rays has a chohan who focuses the God-qualities of the ray for us on earth. See the chart on page 210, Appendix A, for their names, an idea of what each one teaches, and the locations of their retreats.

Christ Self. The universal Christ individualized as the true identity of the soul; the Higher Self, or Real Self, of every man, woman, and child; the Mediator between the soul and her I AM Presence; our own personal teacher, guardian, and friend; the voice of conscience. See the Chart of Your Divine Self on page 176.

Deathless solar body. The spiritual garment of light that is spun out of the light of the I AM Presence as one consciously calls forth the holy energies of God. These purified energies are woven as a seamless garment to envelop the soul in preparation to merge with her Christ Self in the ritual of the ascension. Also called the wedding garment.

Devachan. Tibetan, "blissful realm" or "pure land"; corresponds to the Mahayanic *sukhāvatī* or the Hindu *devaloka* or *svarga*. The first three levels of the heaven-world, a realm of wish-fufillment where a soul may experience her good karma while her negative karma is set aside between incarnations. See page 51, chapter 3, "The Beginning of Heaven" for more.

Etheric octave or etheric plane. The highest plane in the dimensions of Matter; a plane that is as concrete and real as the physical plane but is experienced through the senses of the soul in a dimension and a consciousness beyond physical awareness. It is the world of ascended masters and their retreats and of etheric cities of light where souls of a higher order of evolution abide between incarnations.

Four lower bodies. The four sheaths that surround the soul (the physical, emotional, mental and etheric bodies), providing vehicles for the soul in her journey through time and space. See page 57, chapter 3 "The Soul's Vehicles" for more.

Great Central Sun. The center of cosmos; the point of integration of the Spirit-Matter cosmos; the point of origin of all physical-spiritual creation.

Great White Brotherhood. A spiritual fraternity of ascended masters, archangels and other advanced spiritual beings; spiritual order of Western saints and Eastern adepts who have transcended the cycles of karma and rebirth and reunited with the Spirit of the living God. The word *white* refers not to race but to the aura of white light, the halo that surrounds these immortals. They work with earnest seekers of every race, religion, and walk of life to assist humanity.

Hierarchy. The ladder of life whereby God steps down the power of his universal being through the chain of evolving life. The level of one's spiritual-physical attainment, measured by one's balanced self-awareness and demonstration of the use of God's law by his love in the Spirit-Matter cosmos is the criterion establishing one's placement in the spiritual hierarchy.

I AM Presence. The I AM THAT I AM; the individualized Presence of God focused for each individual soul; the God-identity of the individual. See the top figure in the Chart of Your Divine Self on page 176.

Lords of Karma. The beings of light who adjudicate karma, mercy, and judgment on behalf of every soul. All souls pass before the Karmic Board before and after each incarnation on earth to review how opportunities were used and what future opportunities may be offered. The Lords of Karma have access to the complete records of every soul's incarnations. The Karmic Board acts in consonance with the unconditional love of the I AM Presence and Christ Self of each soul to determine when the soul has earned the right to be free from the wheel of karma and the round of rebirth.

Maitreya. The name Maitreya is derived from the Sanskrit *maitrī* ("friendliness"). Maitreya is the Cosmic Christ, who has also passed the initiations of the Buddha. He is the long-awaited Coming Buddha who has come to teach all who have departed from the way of the Great Guru, Sanat Kumara, from whose lineage both he and Gautama Buddha descended. There have been numerous Buddhas in the history of our earth who have served the evolutions of humanity through the steps and stages of the path of the bodhisattva.

Matter or **Mater.** Latin, "mother." Matter is the feminine polarity of the masculine Spirit. In this context, the entire material cosmos becomes the womb of creation into which Spirit projects the energies of life. Matter is the abiding place of evolving souls.

Rays. The light emanations of the Godhead. The seven rays of the white light which emerge through the prism of the Christ consciousness are (in order from one through seven): blue, yellow, pink, white, green, purple and gold with ruby flecks, and violet.

Retreat. A focus of the Great White Brotherhood, usually on the etheric plane, where the ascended masters preside. Retreats anchor one or more flames of the Godhead as well as the momentum of the masters' service and attainment for the balance of light in the four lower bodies of a planet and its evolutions. Some retreats are open to unascended souls, who may journey to these focuses in their etheric body between their incarnations on earth and in their finer bodies during sleep.

Science of the spoken Word. The science of invoking the light of God to produce constructive change in oneself and in the world. This science is demonstrated through the use of decrees, affirmations, prayers, and mantras to draw down the essence of the sacred fire through the Christ Self, the I AM Presence, and heavenly beings into spiritual, mental, and physical conditions.

Threefold flame. The divine spark that burns in a place separate from the physical heart within the secret chamber of the heart, literally a spark of sacred fire from God's own heart. Also called the Christ flame, it is the soul's point of contact with the Supreme Source of all life. The threefold flame has three plumes: the blue plume of God's power to the left, the yellow plume of God's wisdom in the center, and the pink plume of God's love to the right. Every threefold flame differs in its power, its energy, its size, and whether or not it is balanced, depending upon one's individualization of the flame.

Reincarnation

The Missing Link in Christianity

This groundbreaking work makes the case that Jesus taught reincarnation. Elizabeth Clare Prophet traces the history of reincarnation in Christianity—from Jesus and early Christians through Church councils and the persecution of so-called heretics. Using the latest scholarship and evidence from the Dead Sea Scrolls and Gnostic texts, she also argues persuasively that Jesus was a mystic who taught that our destiny is to unite with the God within. Your view of Jesus—and of Christianity—will never be the same.

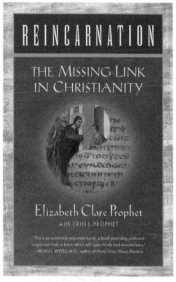

432 PAGES
ISBN 978-0-922729-27-2

Karma and Reincarnation

Transcending Your Past, Transforming Your Future

The word *karma* has made it into the mainstream. But not everyone knows what it really means or how to deal with it. This insightful book will help you come to grips with karmic connections from past lives that have helped create the circumstances of your life today.

You'll discover how your actions in past lives—good and bad—affect which family you're born into, who you're attracted to, and why some people put you on edge. You'll learn

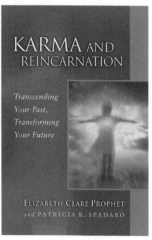

224 PAGES
ISBN 978-0-922729-61-6

about group karma, what we do between lives, and what the great lights of East and West, including Jesus, have to say about karma and reincarnation. Most of all, you'll find out how to turn your karmic encounters into grand opportunities to shape the future you want.

ELIZABETH CLARE PROPHET is a world-renowned author, spiritual teacher, and pioneer in practical spirituality. Her groundbreaking books have been published in more than thirty languages and over three million copies have been sold worldwide.

For more information about Elizabeth Clare Prophet's work, including her Pocket Guides to Practical Spirituality and her series on the Lost Teachings of Jesus and the Mystical Paths of the World's Religions, visit Summit UniversityPress.com.